Seven Decades of Mountain Climbing

A Flatlander's Journey to the Summit

Rod Harris

ISBN: 1-4528-0308-0
ISBN-13: 9781452803081

ACKNOWLEGMENTS

Memory is one of our God-given gifts. I wanted this account to be as accurate as possible, and where memory didn't serve, I was able to rely on many sources. I checked past records from several issues of the *The Chicago Mountaineer.* I also checked Orrin Bonney's guidebook for the climbs I did in the Wind Rivers and their altitudes. For the Teton climbs, I referred to *A Climbers Guide to the Tet* on Range , by Leigh Ortenburger. For the Canadian climbs, *The Iowa Mountaineer Journal.* For Maligne Lake, Jim Hagens report. For the Sawtooth Outing, George Porkney sent me the trip reports. For the Japanese climbs, a Japanese guidebook. For the Everest trek: *The Lonely Planet Guide*, for spelling of villages. And also the personal notes I kept each day on the climbs.

I would like to acknowledge my sincere gratitude to Felix Hagerman who did most of the planning for our early climbs, and shared my enthusiasm for the mountains. Most of all, I want to thank my wife, Lenora, for many hours of typing, and for the many suggestions that made this book possible. Last but not least, I would like to thank my niece, Michele, for all of her knowledge and creative talents in making this book bloom.

THAT FIRST BRUSH WITH DANGER

In August of 1953, at the age of twenty-five, I drove out from Sullivan, Illinois to Lonesome Lake, Wyoming with the Chicago Mountaineering Club. Along the way, my friend Felix and I picked up another member named Harry. Harry had some strange ideas, like never thanking a waitress for bringing you extra coffee because "that's just her job." But he helped out on expenses and part of the driving. I had gotten interested in climbing a few years earlier, but when it came to equipment I had to borrow or live without. By this trip, I had finally bought a small tent and ice axe.

When we arrived, we left our car at Dickerson Park and ventured out on a thirteen-mile hike. We took sleeping bags and extra clothing. The club allowed fifty pounds of gear for each person on packhorses and they furnished breakfast and dinner for the cost of seventy five dollars.

Lonesome Lake is surrounded full-circle by snow-covered peaks of jagged rocks with unbelievable views in all directions. That first day we attended a snow climbing school where they taught us to stop falls and cut steps and I got to use my new ice axe.

Paul Stettner, was the outing chairman. He and his brother Joe were the first to climb Stettners Ledges (regarded as the hardest multi-pitch alpine route in Colorado for many years). It was a joy to see Paul on the snow; his demonstrations were awesome. He showed us self-arrest, which is using the ice axe to dig in and stop a fall. Also how to glissade, which is essentially sliding down the mountain, using the ice axe for balance. He showed how to do it from every angle and direction. It was a great way to start the outing.

The club hired a cook that supplied breakfast and supper with a buffet table where you fixed your own lunch. They had a big campfire every night with a lot of songs. It seemed like half of us were of German ancestry, so few songs were in English. I will never forget hearing Paul Stettner singing Braham's Lullaby in his soft German voice. When I hear Christopher Plummer sing Edelweiss in Sound of Music, I am reminded of this.

The next day, a group of us climbed War Bonnet. It is a beautiful mountain with formations shaped like feathers. Part way up, a shower of rock came down and we took shelter behind a huge boulder. Unfortunately, Harry still had his ice axe extended and was still exposed. One of the rock missiles struck it and broke a bone in his hand. We would have to return to camp.

The next day, a large group of us climbed Mount Mitchell (12, 482 ft), which is a series of grassy ledges with a great view of War Bonnet.

One of the gals was a high school Botany teacher and she taught us about plants around timberline. Peggy pointed out that trees get shorter and shorter finally becoming little trees about six inches tall and finally none at all due to the thinning of oxygen. She also gave us names of wildflowers along the path, such as the red of Indian paintbrush, the purple of wild geranium, the white lupine and of course all colors of columbine. This would be the beginning of my lifelong interest in mountain flora.

When we got to the top, the view from the peak was breathtaking with exposure in all directions. I could see a long way to the south, clear to Mount Temple with a good view of the Cirque Towers and its many peaks. To the North there lay mountains as far as the eye could see. To the West, Paul Stettner was climbing the east face of War Bonnet with his son, and another friend. It was the most difficult climb of the range. The guidebooks say you should have considerable experience in route-finding before attempting it. It is straight up with very few handholds. Further complicating matters, Paul ended up dropping his piton hammer, so the last three pitches on his way to the top were without protection.

After a day's rest, we decided to try War Bonnet again, but this time, without injured Harry. It wasn't an enjoyable climb because we were spooked about falling rock and had to climb broken rock fragments called "scree," but we did make it to the top of the 12,369 foot summit and registered. We received a "first ascent" in Orrin Bonney's guidebook for this route (the next year when we met the author and climbing veteran himself, Orrin told us he had tried that very same climb, but had been stopped when a large boulder came down and scared them off the mountain). We felt pretty good to be on top of a mountain. After putting forth all this effort and having to rest several times, there is a great joy or elation when you finally get to the top.

This is what makes climbing so enjoyable. After a short stay on top we came down the back way in time for supper.

I also climbed a huge rock formation called Wolfs Head, which was an easy climb we could rappel from. The beautiful wildflowers increased our enjoyment. Along the way we enjoyed the wildflowers—Parry's Primrose, yellow and purple violets growing right out of the snow.

Since we were beginners, we were to go out with club members. But they eventually let us take a party out. We decided to climb Pingora, which looks like a huge stump, not unlike Devil's Tower. Meanwhile a fellow named Karl was taking two beginning climbers up the east face of War Bonnet. Karl had a chip on his shoulder because he was in Germany during World War II. He also had his own way of tying in, which would literally prove to be his downfall. The right way to tie in was around the waist which is the smallest part of the torso. He tied around his chest.

On the trek over to Pingora, we heard cries for help. It was Karl's climbers. His rope had slipped over his head and he had plummeted. We hiked over to the base of the climb and found Karl dead, his parka covering his upper body and head.

A packer walked a horse up to carry Karl down. They placed him in a snowdrift until the rangers could arrive to write up a report. But there was still the matter of the two beginning climbers stuck high above. Since Paul Stettner had climbed the face of War Bonnet, he wanted to duplicate it. He had to go up the backside and rappel down to the two climbers to rescue them. Paul was very upset, because he had tried to convince Karl to change the way he tied in and since he was outing chairman he thought it was his fault. He didn't want the club to get the reputation of being negligent. With only a couple of days left for us at Lonesome Lake, we decided to stay in camp. But the bad luck was not over. The next day Paul's son was riding a horse bareback and fell and broke his arm.

The news of Karl's fatality made the *Chicago Tribune*, so we knew our parents back home would read it. Once we got back to phone lines, we assured our families we were fine.

As the trip wound to a close, we drove down to Estes Park, Colorado and stayed at the Crags Lodge. I climbed Alexander's Chimney on the East Face of Longs Peak with our friend Jim Fisk. Jim was working at the Crags and had climbed it before, but didn't think he could lead it. It wasn't too hard, but there was a lot of exposure. We took a large group of the staff at the Crags up the North Face of Longs. We also climbed a lot on the Twin Owls the last few days before going home.

So there were, having faced death, a broken hand, a broken arm. It had all impressed upon Felix and me the dangers of climbing.

But we were just getting started.

HOW I MET THE MOUNTAINS

It was August of 1947 and I was nineteen years old. Felix's Aunts, Leah and Grace, wanted to head out to Estes Park, Colorado for their hay fever. They offered to pay our hotel bill if we would drive them the 1,100 miles.

It was a nice ride in the new 1947 Desoto, and because I had never been out of Illinois, the scenery changed very quickly. After crossing the Mississippi, the rolling hills seemed endless. The corn fields soon vanished; replaced by meadows of grazing cattle. We stopped for lunch every day; people had sent the Aunts off with cookies and snacks, so we would pull over by the side of the road to eat. We would buy milk and that would be our lunch. I can still picture the Aunts sitting on a blanket, in the grass, eating in the shade of a tree. They were very interested in giving us the real impact of being "Out West" for the first time. Since I had never seen real mountains, they wanted to wait and drive up to them in the morning. We stayed in the relative low country of Greeley, Colorado the second night with this in mind.

That next morning as we drove, the Rocky Mountains slowly came into view along the horizon. Of course, they looked just like the pictures I had seen in books only now they filled my vision. Long's Peak with its big flat top looms above the rest. The morning sun hit the peaks and exposed the snow fields and green valleys that seemed to stretch out endlessly.

We made our way up Big Thompson Canyon. In those days, the road was very narrow with steep cliffs on both sides and sharp curves. A few houses sat perched high up in the cliffs. The road followed along the banks of a rapid moving river, which wound around huge boulders.

The Aunts had reservations at the Crags Lodge in the main building, which was a huge three-story wooden frame building. It had a large dining room, living room, and a library on the main floor. The sleeping rooms were on the second floor, and that is where we stayed. The employees stayed in dormitories on the lower level. The lodge is a place I would come to know almost as well as home, and a place where Felix and I made lifelong friends including the owners. We ate our meals in the dining room since they were included with the cost of the room. The lodge was up the hill from the village. We could really feel the altitude as it was surprising how quickly we ran out of breath for Estes Park is 7800 feet high. Felix and I were soon riding horses to see the backcountry.

One day we drove the car over Trail Ridge Road to Grand Lake. At 12,000 feet, this was as high as I had ever been. There was still a lot of snow on top and we took pictures, throwing snowballs and such. Grand Lake is a small town on a large lake with homes around it. We ate lunch and started back up over Trail Ridge road. Another day we took a trip down to Colorado Springs, a tourist town with all the usual shops and the Garden of the Gods park with its massive red rock formations. Aunt Grace actually had a movie camera and recorded Felix and I climbing on the jagged outcroppings. I guess that was the introduction to my climbing career.

The next day, we received word that Rufus, their brother, had died. So we returned home in about 12 hours when it had taken three days to get there. This trip was enough to get our interest in the mountains and we wanted to go back.

The next year Felix had received a black 1940 Packard convertible for his birthday. We took it and went back to the mountains. It was a classic car, with leather seats. With one flaw, when we stopped for gas the first time, it was two quarts low on oil. It cost almost as much to buy oil as it did gas.

We drove out on Route 2 with its many towns, curves and stop signs. It had looked like a direct route on the map but didn't prove to be. This was the last time we went that way or stayed in a motel. After this, we either drove straight through or camped along the side of the road. We stayed at the Crags and made friends with some guys from Oklahoma. They had a band that consisted of a banjo, tuba and piano, and played in bars all over town. College kids worked at the hotel and it seemed like the help had more fun than the guests. We took hikes and horseback rides with them, which added a lot to our stay.

After seeing Longs Peak every day, we decided to climb it.

The peak, which is 14,255 feet high, was named for Major Steven H. Long in 1820. He saw this huge mountain with a flat top and a notch on one side. It looms above all the mountains around it.

There was a horse stable at the beginning of the trail, where we could rent horses so we rode to the start of the boulder field. There was a hitching rack there with a water trough. At this time we found cables at the difficult sections, so it was a long hard scramble to the top. The park rangers have since taken the cables down to make the climb more natural. The top was a surprise to me, because it was a big flat area about the size of a football field. It had a single high point, with a register there, so we signed into our first summit on July 24th, 1948. I was twenty years old.

Since this was our first view from the top of a mountain, we were awed to see Pike's Peak from up there with its snowy top 150 miles away and the many mountains to the west.

After a short time, we started down. In those days, everyone went down a backside path known as the Key Hole route, because it was supposed to be easier. It was a long way around and was the last time we ever did it. We decided it was better to go straight down, the same way we had gone up. After about two hours, we finally found our horses and started down. It began raining, so we had to stop and put on our rain slickers, which were supplied on the back of the saddle, just like in the movies. We did pretty well, but the horses didn't like it at all, especially when they had to face the wind on the switchbacks. By the time we got back to the stable, it had quit raining. This climb was clearly the high point of our trip in more ways than one. We had big stories to tell everyone when we got to the lodge. When we called home Felix's Father told him, he would pay for us to stay another week. We spent that week riding horses all around the area, going up to the meadows among the wildflowers and streams.

I didn't get back to the mountains until 1952. My friends, Ron, Evan, my brother Gordon, and I took a circle trip to the West. We drove straight through to Rapid City, South Dakota, with a brief stop at the Badlands. We got there in time to see a real rodeo, but it was hot and the area is dry and we were so tired, we weren't very impressed. The next day we drove to Devil's Tower in Wyoming. Evan's brother Alan and his wife Celia, friends from home, had told us to be sure to stop and see it. We climbed up the boulder field to the base of the climb, never dreaming Felix and I would climb the tower four years later. We had been told to enter the Grand Teton National Park from the North, so we drove through Wyoming to Dubois. That night we found a wheat field that had just been harvested, so there was plenty of straw to make a soft place to sleep. We were so close to the road, we heard trucks going by all night long.

I don't think you can prepare yourself for the jagged, snowy, outline of the Tetons. They seem to pop up from the valley floor. The Grand Teton, at 13,770 feet, is probably the most photographed mountain in the country. When you see a mountain scene in advertising, it is probably the Tetons with the Grand in the center. We stopped at the first turnoff and took a lot of pictures. As we got closer, Jackson Lake, and the Snake River came into view. We soon made our way to Jenny Lake, a small lake hidden in the forest with a campground at the edge, and set up camp. Felix had climbed the Grand Teton earlier that summer and he highly recommended that we do it.

But first we were required to attend a climbing school for belay, rappelling and signaling. Our instructor was none other than Willie Unsoel, a well-known climber who would later have a First Accent on of the West Ridge route of Everest. He took us out to an area reserved for the school and we practiced belay and rappelling. A belay is when one climber, in a secure spot, fastens a rope to another climber for safety. Rappelling is when you drape the rope around your body and slide down. The signals are so the whole party understands what are in process. Rope in those days was goldline nylon that was invented in the Second World War and since then has been replaced by a much more flexible nylon.

The next day the four of us plus our guide Bob Merriam started up the long trail to the area known as Lower Saddle. The Exum School of Mountaineering had a large tent up there. I had never been so tired as I was when we got there. Gordon, Evan, and I just ate some soup and collapsed, but Ronnie (age 16) and our guide went over and climbed the Middle Teton. We got up around 4 o'clock the next morning and had some hot chocolate. We then hiked through a lot of scree with just a trace of a trail to Wall Street. It was starting to get light, the sun shinning on the side of the Middle Teton. This is called Alpenglow, when the sun hits the peak of the mountain and turns it to gold. A spectacular sight!

Wall Street is a famous step-over of about three feet that is the key to Exum Ridge. We could look down through our legs for about one thousand feet. This is where you rope up. The climb was not hard, but there was a lot of "exposure" as they say, with vast sheer walls of rock above and below as you climb. When you reach the top, it is just a big boulder with a register where we all signed in. We really felt like we were on top of a mountain and it was great. We enjoyed the view, shook hands, and stayed long enough to eat lunch. On the way down there was a hundred foot rappel which was pretty thrilling for us because we had only rappelled at the school. We did have ropes tied around us on a belay so it was relatively safe but rappelling in those days was a bit more dangerous than today. We didn't have the equipment that they have now, it was strictly body rappels and there was always danger of the rope slipping and giving you a bad burn. I think every climber had that happen at least once.

I had rented some boots and sunglasses. One boot had a nail that stuck into my heel, so I was limping by the time we got down. In those days we cut the switchbacks by going straight down instead of going back and forth, so we were going fast which made the heel hurt worse. The sunglasses gave me a headache, so I was in bad shape by the time we got down. After a meal at the Chuck Wagon and a nice sleep, I was okay again.

The next day we packed up and headed for Jackson and took in the sights. This is a real western town, with a small park in the center and on each corner, was an arch of elk antlers. In the front of the businesses were the old boardwalks. Most everyone was wearing cowboy boots and hats which added to the atmosphere. We then drove down to Estes Park and camped at a National Park campground. We looked up Felix Hagerman that was working at a lodge in the Valley. He had been practicing climbing and was all excited about it. We climbed Twin Owls together and decided to climb the East Face of Longs. Gordon, Evan, and Ronnie wanted to go to Colorado Springs and since I had been there, I stayed in Estes with Felix. At the Lodge there was a guide named Otto Von Allmen that would take the two of us up the East Face of Longs for forty dollars a piece.

The route was called Stettners' Ledges and was the hardest climb on the east face that the guides would take parties up. It was a great climb of about one thousand feet of sheer wall. I didn't have any boots, so I climbed in white buck shoes. I had tennis shoes, but they said the buck shoes would be better since there was a lot of snow at the beginning of the climb. We left about five in the morning and hiked up to Chasm Lake. The rock climb began around the lake at the highest point of the snow field. It was almost straight up from there on, so we roped up. There was a place with a horizontal crack about twenty feet across with five pitons (metal pegs) about three or four feet apart. I was last on the rope, so I had to collect the carabineers. I had to unsnap the carabineer while holding on with one hand. To me this was the hardest part of the climb. We soon got to "Broadway" which is a ledge four or five feet wide, clear across the upper part of the face. It is mostly a scramble from there on. We stayed roped up clear to the top, which was the last time we ever did that. By eleven o'clock, we signed in and clearly stated we had climbed Stettners' Ledges. It is a climb you remember the rest of your life, a definite milestone, a feeling of exhilaration, something you just have to feel for yourself. We came down the North Face and since we were taking short cuts on the switchbacks we got down to the car early.

The next day, Felix drove me down to the Brown Palace Hotel in Denver where we met the other guys, and I rode back to Sullivan with them.

That autumn, my brother Gordon and I had bought a new Pontiac, so we took our whole family down to the Smokey Mountains in Tennessee. Gordon and Janice and I took a short trail to the top of Clingman's Dome, which was the highest point in Tennessee, (6,433 ft). The trees had all changed and the scenery was gorgeous, the rolling hills bursting with color in all direction. We spent the week-end driving through the countryside, in our new car, through all the small towns.

THE CHICAGO MOUNTAINEERING CLUB

I had read a book *Annapurna* written by Maurice Herzog, which describes his first ascent of the highest Himalayan Mountain climbed in that era. The author came to Chicago with a slide show and Felix and I drove up there to see it. Maurice had lost most of his fingers and part of his toes to frostbite, so it was quite gruesome.

The most important thing to come out of the event was meeting Paul Stettner, the man who would later rescue those climbers up on War Bonnet. We found out he and his brother Joe were originally from Germany and had done extensive climbing in Europe and the Tetons. Felix had noticed he was wearing a Chicago Mountaineering pin, so he introduced himself and we learned all about the mountaineering club. We told him about having climbed Stettners Ledges and he invited us to come up to Mississippi Palisades in the spring.

That next April, we drove up to the Palisades, on a Friday night. We didn't have tents, so we slept out in the open. The next morning we got up and met all the members of the club. The Palisades has a lot of sandstone rock formations and several cliffs. We soon were practicing three points of contact, and not using our knees. We had to drive home that night, but we knew we were going to go to Devil's Lake in two weeks.

After work, Felix and I and our friend Bill drove the 300 miles to Wisconsin. There were no designated camp sights, so we camped in the trees by the railroad where we met a man named Jim Toler and began a lifelong friendship. Jim had been a bomber pilot in the Second World War, and had many stories and told some of the bad sand storms in the Sahara Desert. His humor and his outlook on life made him a real asset to the group.

We started going to Devil's Lake, every two weeks, with usually four or five from town and became known as, "the Sullivan Boys." The lake is forty-five feet deep and is fed by springs making the water clean and cold. It is surrounded by rock cliffs and therefore a great place to practice rock climbing, with over a thousand routes described in the guidebooks.

So the fall of 1953 was filled with climbs at the Palisades and Devil's Lake. We were taking parties out and got in a lot of good climbs, sometimes as many as ten. For each climb, I usually took five or six people and would hike up the boulder field until we got to the bottom of the cliffs and then roped up. It was good practice for the mountains. I would lead up until we had a good belay point, and then bring the next climber up. He would in turn bring the next one up; this was repeated until they were all up, while I would either go on higher or go down and find another climb. This is how we made our way to the top, where we would eat lunch. We would practice rappelling before going back down.

There was a bar in the park called Beir Stube, where we met all the climbers and compared our climbs of the day. There was a beer brewed in Baraboo called Effengers and we did our best to help the local economy. We always drove home Saturday night to be home for church on Sunday morning.

Felix and I decided to go to the Tetons in the summer of 1954. Jim Toler was going to join us out there, but couldn't get off work until the middle of August, so we stopped by Estes for a couple of weeks. We climbed Longs Peak and practice climbed on Twin Owls, so we were in good shape by the time we got to the Tetons. Jim wasn't to arrive for a couple of days, so we decided to climb Nez Perce (11, 901 ft). It is an Indian name meaning howling dog. Its outline looked to them like a howling dog. It is pronounced Nay Pursay, the official name comes directly from the Nez Perce tribe of Indians that hunted in the area. We were on top by nine o'clock, so we climbed on over to South Teton. We climbed the ridge which included Cloudveil, Spaulding, and Gilkey Spire, each one about 12, 000 feet. We had been taught to start down by two o'clock so we did. As we looked back up we saw a long snow field that we could have slid down and we would have gotten down a lot faster if we had just gone over to South Teton. I never did get to climb South Teton and have always been sorry we didn't do it that day.

Jim had taken the train to Victor, Idaho, so we drove over Teton Pass to pick him up. This was a beautiful drive in those days with a lot of sharp turns and steep curves. We were camping at Jenny Lake campground where all the climbers stayed. The next day we climbed Symmetry Spire (10, 560 ft) by the East Ridge. The guide book says this is the most enjoyable way to the top. You don't need a rope up. It has grassy ledges with good views of the lakes in hanging canyons. On the way down, Felix and I climbed Storm (10, 054 feet) and Ice points while Jim waited on the saddle. Storm point gives the finest view in the park of the Cathedral group.

The next day we climbed an impressive mountain, Teewinot (12,325ft), by the east face. Teewinot is the Shoshone Indian name meaning pinnacles. The East Face is the one you see from the campground and from this angle; looks like the highest peak in the park and is commonly mistaken for the Grand Teton. It seemed like the hardest part of the climb was to get to the base of the mountain. You have to go through a meadow with lots of low water and wildflowers shoulder high. The actual climb is up loose rock with not much of a trail. You try to find the most stable footing. The last part is good rock and does come to a point at the top. The guide book says there are eighteen switchbacks, but I think most people go straight up. This is the only mountain I have ever seen that actually comes to a point. Jim had a movie camera and took pictures of us standing on top. We got down without any trouble and were told later, that most of the accidents occur on the way down because they get off the trail and into the loose rock.

The following day we met Orrin Bonney, the guide book author and climbing veteran. A classic eccentric, he had a large teepee sat up in the campground. This is where all the climbers met and since he knew many people in the Chicago Mountaineering Club, it was a great place to meet other climbers. He had been on the outing when Joe Stettner climbed the east face of Monitor and in fact was watching the climb with binoculars. When Joe made the climb it was recognized as the hardest climb in the country. He was impressed that Felix and I had climbed at Lonesome Lake the previous year. He was there in 1940 and had several first ascents. All while we were at the Teepee, famous climbers kept coming by. There was a small campfire in the center of the teepee, so we all went out to Timber Island, a large area east of Jenny Lake that is nothing but sage and gathered dead brush. That night, the burning sage filled the air with a dry, woody and yet sweet aroma that I will forever associate with the mountains.

One day we went over to Paul Pretzel's cabin to meet him, as he was one of the pioneer climbers of the Tetons, he had lots of stories and we just sat there and listened. He had probably told them a hundred times, but they were priceless to us. He had been on the first attempt by the Americans of climbing K2 in Nepal. They had turned around 600 feet from the top and he was still sorry, however most experts think, that's what saved his life.

We wanted to climb something the next day, but the weather was cloudy with threats of rain, so Orrin suggested Templeton's Crack on Symmetry Spire. Jim decided to stay in camp and wash the dishes with soap and hot water, which was probably a good idea. Templeton's Crack was a climb you could do in threatening weather; since there were a lot of places you could find shelter. It was a long scramble blocked by a huge chock stone, then another long scramble and another chock stone. This was repeated three times before you got on the final ridge. We were the only ones that made a summit that day, so we felt pretty good.

The next day it finally cleared up so we decided to try the Grand. This was what we had been looking forward to all summer. We camped at the Caves which were part way up and so we didn't have to bring a tent. We got a late start the next day, and somehow I only brought one rope, which meant for short leads. Felix and I had climbed it before, so we let Jim go first. We made good time after we got on the rock, and were on top by 11 o'clock. We did have to wait on somebody to share a rope for our rappel, but we did get down in good time.

That night we went down to the Cowboy Bar in Jackson to celebrate with our friends. Jackson was a wide open town with gambling everywhere. We couldn't believe all the slot machines, roulette wheels, black jack tables and so forth. The next morning we drove to Estes. I got a job at the Stanley Hotel as a busboy, so we stayed two more weeks and then came home. We didn't get in as much climbing as we would have liked, but we did get to climb the Grand and we had met a lot of famous climbers, so we were glad.

So now our lives were about climbing or planning our next climb.

FIVE MEN, A HEARSE AND A CLOSE CALL

That fall of 1954, we entered into a new era of seriousness in our travels, that is to say we purchased a used hearse. Five of us put in fifty dollars each. This made our trips to the lake much easier. We put a full size mattress in the back, so three people could sleep, with two in front driving. We started going to Devil's Lake in the winter that year. We didn't cook any meals, instead went to Baraboo for breakfast and supper. It was usually nine or ten before we got started climbing and we quit by four, so we didn't get much time on the rock.

The evening meal in the Warren Hotel became the best part of the trips. There were usually about ten or fifteen climbers and after the meal, Paul Stettner Jr. would play his guitar and we would all sing. Finally the whole restaurant would join in and sing. Paul Sr. always requested Felix sing "On Top of Old Smoky." Several years later, the Warren Hotel burnt and left nothing but good memories.

After admiring Orrin Bonney's teepee, Felix and I decided to make one of our own. We obtained a plan and bought some white material. A mechanic in the Sullivan Dress Factory set up a sewing machine for us in the top floor. After two or three Saturdays of one holding the fabric while the other sewed, we finished it and took it to Elim Park. Then we had to find ten long thin trees and cut them into poles. Finally, we had it all together and rejoiced over our accomplishment. It had taken us all winter, but we finally had our Teepee. We left it up all summer. It was a talking point and a sight to see. Some of the young people camped in it and I think I did a few times, but since it wasn't water proof, it wasn't as wonderful as we had envisioned. I don't think any tribe would have adopted us.

Throughout 1955, we continued going up to Devil's Lake. Back then, the south side of the lake was ringed with summer houses. We had a friend who lived in a cottage there and he usually had a new climb for us. Dave was a really good climber. He was always looking for hard places to climb and passed them on to us, often expecting we couldn't manage it. We proved him wrong every time.

That year, The Sullivan Boys (Felix, our friend Peter, my brother Gordon and I), joined the CMC on a trip to the Northern Wind Rivers, where there are more glaciers there than any place else in the country. To get there, we had to go through the Crow Indian Reservation and get permission to climb. The Club had a packer that furnished a cook and took in fifty pounds per climber to the campsite. We drove as far as we could and then a flat bed truck took us to the start of the trail. We could now see Gannett (13, 785 ft), and it looked like a huge ice cream cone. It is the highest point in Wyoming. The campsite was in a big meadow with a lot of pine trees called The Floyd Wilson Meadow. He had tried to set up a climbing service here in the 1940's. There were still remains of teepees, but it failed because it was too hard to get to and the season was too short.

The first day, we climbed Horse Ridge (13,000 ft), which was close and we got a feel for the area. It was not a fun climb, as we mostly climbed scree up a rotten gulley. I climbed Bastion (13,500 ft) next, and was by this time considered a leader and Bastion was a good beginning. We made excellent time since it was close to the camp and we didn't have to go to the glacier. It had a nice chimney near the top that I was able to stem. Rampart was another 13, 000 foot peak that I climbed the next day.

The Club had a rule that everyone had to spend one day in camp, gathering wood for the cook and the evening campfire. I remember we used two-man buck saws to cut up the logs. The logs were then stacked, what was called the Stettner Way, which was laying two largest logs separate and parallel, with two crossing them, then another two across those and so forth, like the old notched Lincoln Logs, making a square on top of square as high as you could reach, with the kindling perched at the top. As it burns the coals fall down into the tower warming and drying the larger logs below, providing a very contained long burning campfire, and if done correctly leaves every piece of wood burnt down to ash. It became a competition to see who could get the highest tower. I still use this method of building even a small campfire and my children and grandchildren have grown up with this.

Felix, Paul Jr. and I climbed Pinnacle Ridge next. It wasn't a true mountain, but a long snow covered ridge with lots of high points, about a mile in length. It was hard to get started because we had to cross a deep crevasse, with several snow bridges so we roped up. We let Paul go first since he was the lightest. We used our ice axes the entire way.

Woodrow Wilson was my next climb. We got up at four a.m., since it was so far away but oatmeal awaited all the early climbers in the cook tent. There was a long glacier approach that forced us to use crampons (metal-spiked footwear) for the first time. We had been told to buy them and we were glad we had them. This was a great climb with snow after the ice and finished up with a nice rock face. When Wilson was first climbed, it was thought to be the highest in Wyoming, but Gannet proved to be higher. We got in so late, that I took a day of rest and did my work day.

Paul Stettner posted a climb up Koven (12, 200 ft) and we all wanted to climb with him. It was a great honor to climb with him and he had a big party of good climbers. It was another early start, up the glacier, and a big snow field and the problem of finding a snow bridge to get to the rock. It was not hard climbing and we got on top real early. As we ate lunch, we spent about an hour, listening to Paul tell stories. There was a long glissade (slide) down the snow, so our boots got cold and wet.

We got home just in time for supper. But it was no feast. The club had hired a cook and gave him money to buy food but he never came back. So they had to hire a new cook and food with what money was left. Supper that night consisted of vegetable soup, followed by stew meat. We were so hungry, we didn't care much, and there were good desserts. Then we sat around the campfire repairing our boots with kits the club had furnished.

Since Gannet Peak was the highest in Wyoming, everyone wanted to climb it. I was lucky and I got to go with Paul Stettner as an assistant. The Green River starts on its snow covered slopes. Colin Fletcher wrote about this in his book called, The River.

We left at five in the morning, stopping by for our oatmeal, and then hiked on up the glacier, in a dense fog. It grew worse as the day wore on. The view was obscured by a fine mist with periods of sleet. I had never climbed in this kind of weather and would probably have turned around if Paul had not been there. Someone asked Paul if we should turn back and he said, "If I did, it would be the first time." We didn't get to sign the register until one in the afternoon. I was really disappointed because we were not able to see the Teton Range. The year before, when we were on top of the Grand we could see Gannet. It was late when we got down, but I was happy since we had climbed the highest mountain in Wyoming and it was with Paul. The club had a good record that year since anyone wanting to climb Gannet was given the opportunity.

We spent the final day in camp cleaning up, because we wanted to leave the camp in better shape than when we got there. That night we had a giant campfire with lots of German songs.

The next morning, Felix, Peter, and I drove down to Estes, Colorado, where Peter and I got jobs at the Crags as busboys. Our main duties were pouring coffee, clearing tables, and carrying trays of food for large parties. We got our afternoons off, so we usually went on practice climbs. One of our friends wanted me to take pictures of him climbing so he could send them to his mother. He wanted me to tilt the camera to make it look like the climb was really hard. Imagine his disappointment when he realized I had tilted the camera the wrong way and the pictures looked like he was crawling on the ground. Other days we played touch football on the High School field which was right downtown.

On our day off, Felix and I decided to climb Stettners Ledges. It was to become one of the more momentous days in my life, but not for any reason I'd have chosen.

We started at the trailhead, up the telephone lines, and were on the Hogback, just as the sun was coming up. There were no mountains in the east, so we could see the sun break the horizon. They say you can see the curvature of the earth there, but I don't remember that. It took us one hour to get to The Hut at Chasm Lake, so we would never carry sleeping bags or extra food. Looking over at the East Face of Longs from here was a 12, 000 foot face that extended east to Mt. Meeker and west to the diamond with total exposure. Awesome, so we really wanted to do it. We walked around the lake and began the climb. We alternated leads, and were on Broadway by 9:30. I happened to be leading the famous Piton Ladder, and I think it was easier than being last. We were feeling really good, thought we could do anything, so we decided to try the window route, a large hole in the face that looked like a window with a lot of exposure.

I led up, found a good belay position and a piton that I used for protection—a good choice it turned out. Felix climbed up to me and on past and soon ran into trouble. He decided he was off the route, so he started back down. He had driven in a piton and was trying to place a sling, so he could rest before trying another route. Just then he slipped. And I will always remember him flying past me with all the rope trailing behind him. We had been taught to wear gloves and let the rope slide before stopping the fall. I had not worn gloves, and the rope burned the palm of my hands as it slid through. He finally stopped after his nearly sixty-foot fall and then yelled up to me, so I knew he was alive. I climbed down and then we went on down to Broadway, rested awhile and collected ourselves.

We met a couple of friends who had been climbing Alexander's Chimney. They had seen our fall. It turned out Felix had a broken wrist and fortunately one of the men had a first aid kit, so he fixed up a temporary splint. Felix also had a bad cut on his knee, so they bandaged that too. They had a small camp stove, and made us some soup to ward off shock.

From there we decided it would be easier to take an easy route to the top of the mountain instead of trying to rappel off the face because Felix was not in shape for the several difficult rappels.

Upon our return we were suddenly famous. The Denver papers had the story and the Associated Press picked it up, so some of the local papers at home picked it up too. Joe Hawks came over from Winter Park on his motorcycle. Hawks had the record up the Grand Teton for many years of five hours and twenty minutes. He and his wife Peggy were high school teachers, so they spent their summers in the mountains every year. His first words were, "What did you do wrong?" To him, it was inexcusable for the leader to fall.

Felix decided to fly back home, but Peter and I stayed for two more weeks and finished out the season in our jobs. By the end of it, we were almost broke, but we did have a sack full of tip money; which we used to buy gas and food on the way home.

BACK ON THE ROPE

That autumn, we returned to Devil's Lake to mixed reactions. Some wished us well, while others thought our luck had finally run out on us. For Christmas vacation we went on a ski trip to Colorado. I enjoyed it, but could never ski fast and most of my friends were better skiers, so I still preferred climbing. Felix had fully recovered from his fall and by the summer of 1956; we were back at Devil's Lake doing a lot of hard practice climbing.

In August, a large group of friends from Sullivan and club members set out to meet in the Tetons. We stopped by Devil's Tower on the way. At that time, you had to have someone recommend you before you could climb the Tower and Joe Stettner did this for us. Joe had led a famous ascent in the forties. When we got there someone else was already signed up to go the next day, so we watched them and learned from their mistakes. The leader wore out a pair of shoes on the small cracks. The next day when it became my turn, I stemmed on the outside, which was a lot faster. Stemming is when you have one foot and hand on an opposing corner of a cliff and have the other on the other side, then make your way up. We had been told that the record time was a little over an hour and a half, so we tried to better this. We got on top in an hour and thirty three minutes, but that same week somebody did it in an hour and twenty nine minutes. The reason we did it so fast was because we didn't have to add any pitons. We just used the ones that were already there. When we got to the top, we found cans of tomato juice that someone had left, and we drank some. This was the first time Felix had ever drank tomato juice, but we were really thirsty after a hard climb. We got down by eight thirty. When I was there years later, I checked the records and found we had been the 276th assent on the Tower.

We then drove over to the Tetons where we met a group from Chicago and some friends from home. When we signed in at the Ranger Station we were teased a lot because they had read the accident report in the American Alpine Club news letter. Felix had written a long account of the fall for the Chicago Mountaineering Newsletter. He had gone into great detail on how we felt before and after. He told of the mistakes we had made and how we could have done it better. The American Alpine Club yearly accident report picked this up and printed the whole thing. Felix had only broken his arm but got more pages than if he'd died.

Our first climb was Nez Perce (11,901ft) to get in shape. The Chicago group only had a week and wanted to climb the Grand, so we went up to the Meadows for a high camp. We had a large group, so we decided to divide the group and one went up the Owen Spalding route, and the other went up the Exum Route. Part way up, we ran into a lightning storm. We could smell the ozone and hear the buzzing sound. The procedure is to get as low as possible and under a rock. That way, if you get struck by lightning, at least you wouldn't compound the problem by falling off a mountainside. We were lucky that the storm didn't last very long. The two groups met on the Summit for a nice celebration.

On the way down, we realized our friend from home, Burnett, had no experience in rappelling. He turned upside down and made the whole descent that way. He was on belay so he wasn't in any danger, but it made for good stories for years to come.

We broke camp, headed down to Jenny Lake and decided to do some sightseeing. We drove to Yellowstone, visited Old Faithful and the other tourist attractions. In those days, everyone fed the bears, so every few miles there would be a bear watch with dozens of cars parked along the side of the road.

Our friend Ollie wanted to do a face climb, so we decided on Symmetry Spire (10, 560 ft) by the Durance Ridge route. We made up a party with Felix and Ollie on one rope and me and another man on the other. It was a 800 foot face with handholds in all the right places up the face and this was a good chance to do it. It wasn't as difficult as Stettner's Ledges, but since we hadn't done it before, it had that unknown quality. We made good time, but got off route when we followed another party that was trying for a new route. They were also trying out a new signaling system. Instead of using the usual signals, such as slack or up rope, they would shout, "Peep" or "Peep Peep." Needless to say, this system was never adopted by the climbing community.

We got on top early and came down by the standard route. Ollie and the Chicago group had to leave, so Felix and I, my brother Gordon, and our friend Peter went up to Amphitheater Lake to try the East Ridges of the

Grand and Mount Owen (13,058 ft). After setting up camp, we watched a party on Disappointment Peak, coming down the big snow field, when suddenly one of them slipped and slid into the rocks. Since there were several in the party, we felt they could handle the problem. Later that evening, rangers came up with a stretcher since the climber had broken his leg.

Next morning, we started up the East Ridge of the Grand. After going across the moraine, we scrambled up the easy rocks, until we got to the base of the Molar Tooth. We then roped up, with Felix and Gordon on one line, and Peter and I on the other. We went around to the north, where you get a great view of the legendary North Face. This is the most famous North Face in the United States and the goal of most climbers. Then you have to rappel past an icy gulley. We were following guidebooks closely now and this particular gulley was often filled with snow, but we were lucky to find this time it wasn't.

The climb up to the second tower was the hardest part. It was smooth rock with patches of snow for two or three hours. Going across the north side we saw the summit snow field, where ice axes were very handy. The snow was pockmarked like the surface of the moon, with large craters about three feet across and a foot deep, the result of the sun reflecting.

There was a huge boulder on top which we bypassed on the North. We didn't stay long, rappelled down, and were soon at the top of Teepee Glacier, which ends up near our camp. There was about a foot of new snow, which made for slow going. It was very steep, so we belayed down and finally got back in camp. It was the steepest snow I had ever been on, so we were glad to get back to our tents.

After a rest day, we decided to climb the East Ridge of Mount Owen. There is a long walk across the moraine, just below the North Face, so you get a good view of it. As we were resting, a big boulder came down the gully we were about to climb. Thinking back, it seemed like it was about the size of a box car, but age has probably made it bigger. We had been told to climb the left side of the gulley and this proved that point.

Mount Owen (13,058ft) is a very beautiful mountain with many snow fields, perhaps the most beautiful in the Tetons. At the top of the gulley, the ridge starts with very hard rock climbing with very little hand holds. At one point, my ice axe which was in my pack, got stuck in an overhang, so I had to back down to release it. It was hard going up, but it was harder backing down due to the tremendous exposure involved. The whole climb was very tricky with the snow being the easiest part, but we did finally get on top. We came down the Koven Route, which has been the most popular route on the mountain since it is the least difficult.

After getting back to our camp, we packed up and headed down to Jenny Lake, where we met Alan and Celia, friends from home. We decided to go out and take pictures, so we went up the east ridge of Disappointment Peak keeping our string of East Ridges going. We took a lot of pictures since there was no pressure and we could just take our time.

We then went down to Estes and the Crags, where I got a job again as a busboy. On my day off, I took a party of five boys that worked there, up Longs Peak. We made very good time, and spent about two hours on top. It was fun to watch people come up to that summit and have that experience with all different points of view. About thirty years later, I got a letter from one of those five boys telling me that day on Long's was the most exciting thing he had ever done. He had seen the north face of Longs Peak written up in a travel section of a newspaper and wanted to know if that was what we had climbed. I was glad to tell him that it was and thanked him for remembering. I have had a lot of people tell me similar stories.

The Sullivan Boys climbed all winter at Devil's Lake again. During one trip a cattle truck ran a stop sign and we crashed into its side, totaling the hearse. Since it had cost only two hundred and fifty dollars, the truck owner was glad to pay for it. So we purchased another and were really just very thankful no one was hurt. We bought a 1948 black Cadillac this time and it would prove to have its own interesting stories.

On a ski trip to Wisconsin, our friend Steve broke his leg and he stayed in the hearse while we went into a restaurant for supper. We asked the waitress to prepare something to take out to him. As he was sitting up in the back, eating his supper, a lot of passersby were greatly amused. On another trip, we had to make a sudden stop, and lost all the brake fluid, so driving was very hard and got much worse until the last drivers shift, when there were no brakes at all. Since it was a manual, we would shift down until we were barely coasting and hope no one was coming. I was driving that last shift and I still remember it well.

MY BEST YEAR OF CLIMBING

In 1957, we had signed up with the Chicago Mountaineering Club to go to Lake O'Hara, which is located near Mount Victoria in Alberta, Canada.

Felix and I stopped by the Tetons, where we met my brother, Gordon. We were in the ranger station trying to get a campsite, when we met Barry Corbet, and Jake Breitenbach. They said we could camp with them, since we were only going to be there over night. Later, they were on the 1963 expedition on Mount Everest, when Jake fell to his death.

We felt we were ready to try the North Face of the Grand Teton, which is the most famous route and set up camp at Amphitheater Lake. Then we crossed the moraine to the base of the climb, set a fixed rope at the base of the bergshrund, which was a big crack at the end of the glacier. Sometimes it is difficult to get across one of these. We came back, and the three of us slept in a tiny tent on the glacier. It was really crowded, and sleep was difficult. The next morning, we were able to go back over our fixed rope to the start of the climb.

Felix led to start, paying close attention to the guidebook. He had to make sure he was following the route, as time was a factor and we couldn't afford any false leads. There is a huge snow field in the center that can be seen from the valley below, so we really needed our ice axes. Most of the time we strapped them to our back packs.

When we got to the Pendulum Pitch, which was the crux of the climb, I took over the lead. I climbed a short chimney and Felix came up to belay me. We had to go around a corner to climb the North Face direct. We would never have done that if the guide book had not described it. You go on your hands and knees until you run out of space and then drop down for a hand traverse. Your rope is pulled tight against the face and the guidebook says to put a glove in the crack to keep the rope from getting stuck. I forgot this and had to back up to release the rope. After getting around the corner, there was a nice stance to belay the other climbers from a twenty foot drop. Then I stood on Felix's shoulders to get to the fourth ledge. Gordon then led up to the summit, which we made by six o'clock.

On top we met some other climbers that remarked they would like to make that climb someday, but we never did find out if they did. We were very much in our prime of skills and strength and it had taken us thirteen hours. Now we had to get down.

Since we had trouble in Teepees Glacier the year before, we decided to take the long way around. It was about midnight before we got back to camp. We slept late the next morning, but did get up to the glacier the next morning to pick up our tent. We were really feeling great when we got back to Jenny Lake. After celebrating with Barry and Jake we left for Lake O'Hara in Canada.

We arrived in Banff and found Alan and Celia Dickens, since they were going on the outing with us. We told them our good news about our climbing the North Face. There was a nine mile walk on a level trail and since the club had hired a packer to carry fifty pounds of our personal gear, it was an easy walk. The camp was unusual since it was in two levels. The upper step was where we placed our tents, and the lower level was the cook tents and the dinning tent. They even had teepees that you could rent and some people did, but they didn't seem very satisfactory. They furnished wood, so most people made the mistake of building too large a fire in the teepee which made it really smoky.

Most of our climbs started low, so we had to go down before starting our climb. The first day, most everyone in camp climbed Mount Schaffer (8,832 ft). On the way up, one climber got sick and had to turn around, so I had to go down with him, since we were afraid he might get lost.

I got to climb Mount Ordway (10, 750 ft) with Joe Stettner. I had climbed with Paul, but this was my first time with Joe. He was a joy to watch, making the climb look easy and he just seemed to float up. Joe had lots of first ascents and was the best climber I ever saw. He and Paul made a perfect combination. They were in their fifties when I knew them, and can only imagine what they would have been like in their prime.

Next, I took a bunch of beginners up Little Ordway (9, 695 ft). It was mostly a long snow field with a high point. One of the beginners was a boy about ten named Roger. His parents were middle-aged teachers who had the summers to spend in the mountains and I admired them for trying to raise a son here. It must have worked, as he turned out to be one of the best climbers the Club ever produced. On the way down, we started a small snow slide; it was only about up to our knees but pretty exciting for a ten year old, exciting for me too.

On Wednesday, Felix and I took out a man and his wife from New York that were both doctors, up Park Mountain (9, 650 ft). It seemed like people were beginning to be afraid to go with us, thinking we would try something that was too difficult. We wished we could be more like Joe Stettner and have people trust our abilities. Park Mountain was mostly a big scree slope, with big slabs of rock just ready to fall. We had to be careful to stay on the path so we wouldn't start an avalanche. The climb did go well, with only a few minor rock slides.

Friends from Sullivan came into camp the next day. Jack had pulled his camping trailer up to the head of the trail. He left his wife enjoy the view, while he and another friend, Barbara, hiked the 5 miles up to our camp. We were very surprised to see them. After lunch they turned around and hiked back.

We had a couple of days of bad weather of heavy clouds with rain and sleet, so we waited and then made a big push to climb Mount Victoria (11,364 ft). This is the mountain in the background of all the calendar pictures you see of Lake Louise. If you stand at the hotel and look towards the lake, it is centered perfectly behind the lake draped in snow. It is probably the most photographed mountain in Canada, maybe the world. About half of the climbers wanted to try it and Paul and Joe were going to take up separate parties. It is about an eight hour hike up a snow gulley to the hut of Abbot Pass. Since there were over two dozen people going up, Felix and I waited until afternoon, and it worked out, we followed in footsteps that were already made in the snow. We got a little static when we arrived and probably should have volunteered to kick steps, since it was a lot easier to follow in steps that were already in the snow. There were only beds for eight people, so we had to draw straws for them. I drew last, but happened to get a bed. Looking back, I should have given mine to one of the older men. The people without beds were issued Hudson Bay Blankets and slept on the floor. This hut was built in 1927, and was the highest permanent structure in Canada at this time and was to be the only overnight place before climbing Mount Victoria.

After a breakfast the next day, Paul started out, but there was so much ice, he could only get about 10 feet before he gave up. Most of the climbers decided to go down since we didn't have enough food for two more days. Five of us decided to stay and it was one of the best days I have ever had in the mountains, since Joe was the life of the party with his German accent and his great since of humor. He had one climbing story after another that endeared him to me for life.

It snowed most of the day, and in the afternoon we heard some cries of help. We lined up outside and walked as far as we could while still keeping the person behind us in view. In this way we got to the person calling for help. Friends of Joe's had come up from Lake Louise and were lost. We invited them in for hot chocolate and warmth. After a short time they decided to go down to Lake O'Hara to get out of the bad weather. The next day we all decided to go down since the rock was still icy and too dangerous to be on. We were disappointed we didn't get to climb the mountain, but we did enjoy spending the day with Joe.

The final campfire was built so high that Joe put his daughter on his shoulders to let her light the fire. Marv David was there with his Banjo to lead the singing. He divided the group into sections and we sang "The Lion Sleeps Tonight".

I walked out with Marv David and was surprised to learn that most of his family considered him the black sheep as they were all doctors or lawyers. Marv was a freelance writer who had good times and bad times. At the time of his death he was given a great obituary by the Chicago Tribune.

Felix and I decided to join the Iowa Mountaineers at Maligne Lake. To get to there, we took a boat to an island and then rode an old 1938 Buick Roadster across the island to another boat that took us to the camp. The boat ride was spectacular, with views of mountains that circled the lake. Upon arrival, we were introduced as climbers that had just done the North Face of the Grand Teton.

The next day we climbed two mountains, Carlton (10, 555 ft) and Unwion (10, 772 ft). They were twin peaks that were separated by a large snow field. The snow was so hard, we could use crampons. We went up a valley between them, climbed the first one, and then the other. Felix had on a pair of mirror sun glasses, so we took pictures of the reflection of the snow peaks in the glasses. By this time he had a beard, so it made a nice picture.

When we got back, we hiked up to a high camp, which was about a two hour trek. From there, we could begin a climb of three peaks. We started out in a snowstorm, which grew steadily worse. We reached the summit of Mount McLeod (10, 600 ft). Part of our party turned back, but Felix and I, along with two guides, went on. At this point there was zero visibility, and we found ourselves bumping into snow drifts.

The next mountain was Valad Peak (10, 663 ft). The ascent was a rock climb off the trail. We stopped for lunch and it started to snow harder. We could see Mount Brazeau (11, 385 ft) and decided to go for it. We followed the guides up a fifteen hundred foot scree and ice slope in the footprints of a previous party. Taking time only to sign the register, we hurried down. We soon were involved in snow and fog so thick we couldn't see two feet in front of us. So we just blindly followed the guides. We'd walk along and we couldn't see what was trail and what were snow drifts. It gave us a panicked feeling to be walking and not seeing what you were walking into. We did get back to base camp in time for a great dinner and song fest in the supply tent. We were able to say we had climbed five mountains in three days.

On this trip we met Hans Gmonser, Dan Doody, and Al Auten. Hans was the one that started helicopter skiing later on. Dan and Al were on the 1963 Everest Expedition. We had an exciting boat ride out of camp in the fog. The boatman had operated boats for years, but became totally lost. He finally opened up his pack and got out his compass. Huge rocks were jutting out of the water and I didn't feel the compass would be much help. This was a very unusual climax to an excellent four days.

Once back on the road, we drove up to Jasper, just to see it. In those days it was a small town built around the railroad. We were amazed at the wildflowers blooming in August around the train station and all government buildings. We drove back down to Banff stopping along the way to spend the night at a Canadian Alpine Club Hostel. We were surprised the next morning when they brought us a large wash basin full of hot water. We ate breakfast with a large group of climbers that had all sorts of stories and we added our share. We did get to brag about climbing the North Face of the Grand.

Felix and I drove down to our friend Jim Toler's home in Rawling, Wyoming. We talked him into coming down to Estes for a week. I rode down with him and his daughter Molly, while Felix rode with Jim's wife Marilyn. Molly, being a toddler, cried most of the trip, much to the embarrassment of Jim. When we got to Estes, Jim and I climbed Alexander's Chimney. We started at three in the morning and got back by nine thirty and they were still serving breakfast at the Crags. The hotel had been showing slides of the climb representing it as an all day climb, so it was a surprise to think we could get back in time for breakfast. We spent that week, showing Jim and Marilyn all the things we had told them about, the Crags, the band, the Twin Owls, and The Stanley Hotel, then parted on the weekend and headed back to Illinois.

We spent that fall and winter climbing at Devil's Lake. Tired of the hearse, Felix bought a Volkswagen bus. It got better mileage, but was less comfortable. One of the first of its kind, it had no gas gauge, had manual turn signals and was greatly under-powered. We took it out west over Christmas vacation to ski at Winter Park, and when facing a headwind, we could only go fifteen miles an hour. But it sailed when the wind was at our back.

A NEW LEVEL OF MATURITY

In 1958, Felix and I went to Lonesome Lake with the Iowa Mountaineers. It was a return to the place we had gone to on our first outing in 1953. This year we were on the advanced party to set up the camp. We were now Rope Leaders, so we didn't have to pay and this made us feel we had finally made the big time. This year, we set up the cook and dining tents right on the lake. There was a nice stream where we could fill up our canteens and get water for the cooks. We then dug two latrines in the woods. This was the first year we were allowed chain saws, so we were looking forward to that, but it seemed like ours was broken most of the time. This first week was pretty nice, as all we did was putter around camp and eat. We had been on diets all summer to stay in shape and now we felt we could let up.

The climbers started coming in by the end on the week, and we were glad to see so many from Chicago Mountaineering Club, Ollie Swartling and George Porkorny were among them. Bill Primack was the outing chairman, and was a little eccentric since he made his own shoes. He couldn't stand to have his shoes touch his toes, so his shoes made his feet look like giant duck feet. He was a great climber and had lots of first ascents in spite of his shoes. Ollie Swartling, had come over from Sweden in 1955, and was a regular at Devils Lake. In fact he has written three Devils Lake guide books, and I still see him when I am up there. George Porkney had been on the Lake O'Hara outing and had been one of the five that stayed at Abbot Hut. He was also a Devils Lake climber and we still exchange emails.

Pingora was the first mountain that I took parties on. It is the mountain Felix and I were starting to climb when we got the call for help from Karl's fall. I was glad to finally get to climb it. This mountain had a nice easy rock face with a good flat summit. We made two good rappels and were soon down.

Dan Doody, who we had met at Maligne Lake, was on the staff, and we took a party up Watch Tower (12,288 ft). (Dan would be on the 1963 Everest Expedition, but would later die on a climb of Mount Washington. He was climbing Tuckerman's ravine, in the winter, and the wind was so strong, it blew him off.) Watch Tower is a mountain that looked like an old castle. We went up fields of wildflowers, along patches of snow. In our trip report, that evening at the campfire, we described our trail through bluebells, the patch of Indian Paintbrush, and how we spotted Parry's Primrose coming out of the snow. It seemed most of our reports concerned the flowers, a joke amongst the climbers.

The climb itself was an easy, rock climb straight up between the two towers. We came down through Wisconsin Couloirs, climbing South Watch Tower (12,250 ft) and Pylon (12,378 ft) on the way back. Pylon is usually tackled separately, but since we were going right by, we decided to climb it and add it to our day.

I began sending flowers in my letters back to my girl, Lenora. I had known her all my life, but had been dating her for over a year and I wanted to send her a bit of the mountains.

Ollie had a good camera and he wanted to take pictures of War Bonnet from Mount Mitchell, so we got up a party to do this. He took many prize winners in black and white. The view was tremendous from this angle with Lake Arrowhead down below. This was the same mountain that Peggy Hawks had given me my first lesson in Alpine flowers many years before.

We decided to see if we could get to War Bonnet by going around to the back side. We went around to Wisconsin Couloirs, turned left, up the ridge to the summit. On the way over, we climbed Warrior Peak (12,406 ft), which was merely a high point with a register, so we got to count it as a mountain. When we got to the top of War Bonnet, we sang Happy Birthday to Lenora, since it was her birthday. We had a very strong party, so we made good time. This climb was given credit for a first ascent in Orrin Bonney's Guidebook.

I will always regret not letting Ken Henderson make this climb. He was about sixty years old and I didn't know how long this would take, so I turned him down. Previously, He and Bill Primack had tried to climb the face and had to stay overnight without making it to the top. I think he could have made our climb. I eventually learned he was the famous climber that had written the Handbook on American Mountaineering and had countless first ascents in the Northern Wind Rivers!

Orrin Bonney came over from the Tetons on a visit, bringing his big Airedale dog that carried Orrin's food in a pack on his back. At the campfire that night, we heard wonderful stories from Ken Henderson and Orrin Bonney of their first ascents in the 1930's.

Felix got a first ascent on a peak called Block Tower (12,000 ft) and Dan Dooley got one on Tiger Tower (11,650 ft). While this was going on, I was climbing Shark's Nose (12,050 ft). This was a sharp rock with no snow. The whole area was filled with peaks like this; you could climb in there for a month and not get them all. In fact, there is a mountain there called August Sixteenth that some of our party climbed on that August Sixteenth.

We then packed up and went down to Estes and stayed at the Crags about another week. We didn't climb anything else but practice climbs. We got home by Labor Day, where we found the humidity was almost unbearable.

All spring and summer of 1959 we were back at Devil's Lake.

In August, the Iowa Mountaineers were going to the Bugaboos in Canada, and we got jobs as guides. My brother, Gordon, got time off from work, so he came along too. The outing got off to a sad start. When we arrived, we learned an accident had occurred up on Mount Roundel, the picturesque mountain that overlooks Banff. A group of climbers were on a warm-up climb, scrambling up a path when one of the climbers dislodged a huge rock and it came down and killed her.

We set up a very elaborate camp, and the site was apparently good enough as it is now the site of the Bugaboo Lodge. They had a huge donut-shaped tent with a large hole in the roof for fires. It was for eating and the campfire afterwards. There was even a ping pong table. After a couple of days, we went up on the glacier and set up a high camp. One of my jobs was to carry a two-burner Coleman stove with fuel and also my own tent, gear and sleeping bag. Most of the climbs were to start from this point, so we had another big dining tent there. It turned out we spent a lot of time there as we had very bad weather. The Bugaboos are a spectacular range with rocky spires jutting out of snow fields. The down side was the rain and fog. I only climbed two mountains in the three weeks I was there.

One was called Frenchman's Mountain, and I took a party of several families and enjoyed it very much. It was mostly grass with a little snow near the top. There were Indian paintbrush flowers of every color in the grass—white, purple, red, everywhere. That evening campfire was mostly the children telling about their first climb with great gusto.

Next, we decided to climb Marmalata (9,500 ft). I took a large group that included some of the members of the Colorado Mountaineering Club. It turned out to be a great climb with a nice long snow ridge, where we used crampons. The sky cleared and we got good views of Snow Patch and Bugaboo Spire. These were the mountains we were here to climb but the weather did not cooperate. I was glad we had climbed when we did. On the way down, we glissaded some very steep snow and I was glad our party was as strong as it was, as it was the steepest I had ever done. I probably would not have done it without the encouragement of the Colorado Group. It made the climb something to remember.

Since it rained the next two or three days, we tried to entertain ourselves. We dammed up a brook and made a nice little pond, with a miniature campsite and boat dock. Al Auten, a guide we met a Maligne Lake, designed a chipmunk trap. It was small plank that went out over the water with food out on the end. When the animal got so far out, it would trip and fall into the water. It worked, but didn't cut down much on the population.

One day, Fred Becky came by our camp. He had been among the spires, but due to the weather, came down. His comment was "No mosquitoes, but lots of ice and snow." He was a famous climber from California that had written several books and even mentioned this trip in one of them. After several days of inactivity, we decided to go down to base camp. We packed up and carried everything down. It felt like we were more like pack horses than mountain guides.

On the way back we stopped in Banff and purchased some sweaters knitted by Cowichan Indians. They use natural wool with the lanolin still intact, making them waterproof and warm. At this point in our climbing careers, we were also wearing lederhosen (leather shorts with suspenders), which we had bought from a catalogue in Germany. To top off the attire we wore small-brimmed, high-peaked Tyrolean hats with many, many climbing pins. Other times we would wear berets or knitted caps to complete the look. Yes, we had been influenced by the fashion of our European counterparts.

But it was for practical reasons as well. Climbing in knickers allowed room for the knees to bend and since we were guides now, we needed to look well-traveled.

On the way home we stopped by the Tetons and saw Orrin Bonney. He told us he knew what it was like to have an outing washed out. We stopped at Estes but didn't stay long and got home by Labor Day.

That fall, Felix got engaged to his future wife, Pat. In winter, we went on our annual ski trip to Winter Park. There I looked up the climbers from Colorado that I had met in the Bugaboo's. Jim Toler came down from Rawlings, Wyoming, so we had a large group. The highlight of the trip was this seven mile run that started in the Berthard Pass Lodge parking lot. It started on a huge pile of snow that has been left there by the snow plows. Almost everyone fell—what a way to begin the run of our life. After we got started, it was single file, so you couldn't fall, or the person behind you would plow right into you. I remember I came down really slow, even snowplowing part of the time. But we were really glad we had done it. The Colorado group had planned a trip up a mountain with a ski descent, but after seeing us on our run, decided we weren't up to the challenge.

A climbing party on Longs Peak.

The Sullivan Boys' hearse.

Climbing at Devil's Lake.

Gordon, Rod and Felix in climbing fashion.

Crossing Devil's Doorway.

Workday with the Chicago Mountaineering Club.

Busboys Peter Van Hook and Rod at Crags Lodge.

A much needed rest stop.

Dan Doody and Rod amidst wildflowers.

Pausing for weather.

Rod and Janice Harris heading to Disappointment Peak.

Daughter Jacque's first climb up Sentinel.

Son Jon atop Storm Point.

Climbing school in Colorado.

Namchee Bazaar, gateway to Everest.

Rod trekking with yak.

One of many suspension bridges on the Nepal trek.

Rod with Ama Dablin Peak.

Rod with daughter Allison (right) descending from snowstorm.

The next generation of climbers.

A NEW LIFE

It seemed all the Sullivan Boys were settling down. Felix was married in spring and Lenora and I planned our wedding for July.

For our honeymoon, Lenora and I drove my 1959 Volkswagen Bug clear across Canada to Banff. In Banff we stayed in the Canadian Alpine Hut before going on up to our cabin north of Banff. We had a beautiful view of Johnson Canyon and stayed a week. Then went up to Jasper on a gravel road and once again enjoyed the beautiful flower gardens around all the government buildings and train stations.

We then came down to Red Fish Lake in Idaho, where I had a job guiding for the Iowa Mountaineers. We were on the advanced party, setting up tents and building tables. The Iowa Club had brought out boats to haul equipment across the lake. The boats proved successful and they were used to bring climbers and their duffel. This is the only outing I was ever on where there was not a hike into the campsite. Felix and Pat joined us in camp as he had a job also. It was Pat and Lenora's first outing and that added a lot to the trip. There was a lot of familiar faces such as Whit Borland, Hans Gmoser, Bill Echo, Marvin David, Tommy Robinson, George Porkorny, that were lifelong friends and made for a very nice time.

Our first climb was Mount Heyburn (10,229 ft), this was the most popular climb. We had parties going up it every day. I was one of the leaders on the first day. It was one of the highest, with beautiful views. We rook the Stur Chimney route, and a group of fifteen went up a gravel and scree couloir, which was not much fun. The chimney led to the top with a lot of exposure, which made it a good climb. Because we had a large party, we set up two parallel rappels. When we got down to the scree, we used a glissade effort to get through the couloir. Everyone got down in record time.

We next climbed Grand Mogul (9,724 ft), a mountain close to our camp that had a huge summit. It was climbed the most often, because it was easy with a tremendous view of the Sawtooths. We could see Castle Peak to the east and Mount Heyburn to the south.

The next day, Lenora and I took an all day hike up to Alpine Lake which was right below Alpine Peak. It was really beautiful with mountains all around us and fields of wildflowers of every color.

I took a party up a mountain called Chockstone, which had twin summits. The peak we climbed was only five feet shorter than its twin, so I got razzed a lot for this.

One day, while I was climbing, Pat and Lenora went down to Sun Valley for the day. Neither of them had been there before and they enjoyed seeing places from the movies—the skating rink, pool, skiing area, and gift shops. Another attraction was Stanley, Idaho. This was where they filmed High Noon. Several people reenacted the famous scene where they had the shootout on the main street.

I climbed Grand Aiguilles (9,800ft), a mountain with good rock and sheer walls; many jam cracks, and a hand traverse to make it an interesting mountain. My partner, Hans, led one rope and I led the other. On the way down, we had a one hundred and twenty foot rappel.

Our final climb was Elephant Perch (9,870 ft). The mountain looks like a big saddle and why it was named Elephant Perch no one seemed to know. We took a zigzag course, through grassy ledges and finally rock. We climbed both summits and could find no registers. It had surely been climbed before, but could find no evidence of it. We made our way down and built our final campfire. On the way home, Bill Echo told us to be sure and stop in Sun Valley and see a friend of his, Louis Stur, who was in charge of the bar. He was interested in what the club had done, and we enjoyed swapping stories for a while. At the time, we didn't realize how famous he actually was. He had a lot of first ascents and had written extensively there.

On the way back to Estes we stopped by Jim and Marilyn Toler's in Rawlins, Wyoming and stayed there that night, then on to Estes where we stayed a couple of days and then home.

We spent the next two years building our home, so all climbing was put on hold. Lenora and I had picked out our site and found a plan that my Uncle Butch had. I worked on putting up forms for the floor, and put in all the drains. It was spring of 1961 before we poured the floor. I received help from many friends to lay up the concrete blocks for the walls and put up rafters. I would go to work at my assembly plant job at five o'clock in the morning and then get off at one o'clock and come out and work on the house until dark. By winter, we were able to move into one room while the rest of the house came together.

I went back to Devil's Lake in 1963, and was glad to find I could still climb. Lenora and I only got up there for the Fourth of July and Labor Day. We did this again in 1964 but we did make it to the Tetons. There was a large group of Sullivan people out there that year. One night we all went down to Jenny Lake to a sing-along. It was called the Teton Tea Party and was hosted by Bill Briggs (the first man to ski down the Grand Teton). I was glad my Sullivan friends could experience this. There was a huge pot on the fire full of a "Tea" which contained much wine. It was dipped out and given to everyone to warm us. Orrin Bonney was there and added a lot to the party atmosphere.

The next day we all climbed up to Amphitheater Lake. My sister, Janice, and I went on up to Disappointment Peak. She didn't quite make it, but I did and was surprised at the exhilaration, these were the same feelings I had had in the mountains.

The next week my Uncle Butch and Aunt Marion brought their sixteen year old son, Joseph, out camping. We decided to take the Teton Crest Trail to Lake Solitude. We started at Leigh Lake, up Indian Paintbrush Canyon, across the Paintbrush Divide through a snow field, where we used ice axes. My sixty-year old uncle had to stop at Holly Lake, but met us down below. It was a twelve-hour hike, but it was well worth it. Years later, Joseph told me it was the best hike he had ever done.

Many of our Sullivan friends had their camps at Coulter Bay, so we had several meals together. Our friend Jack went berry-picking, and his wife, Eileen, made jam on a camp stove.

Meanwhile, the movie studios were filming Spencer's Mountain, with Henry Fonda and Maureen O'Hara, so Lenora and I drove over across the Snake Rive to a small pine forest where they had the movie lot set up and watched the filming. We saw the tree fall on Grandpa, and Maureen sing at the funeral. We were close to all the action, took several pictures of the stars, and couldn't wait for the movie to come out.

In August of 1965, Lenora and I went on an outing to Southern Wind Rivers in Wyoming with the Chicago Mountaineering Club. We had bought the first Ford Mustang sold in Sullivan and were really excited about the drive. We came in from Pinedale, up to Big Sandy Lodge where we stayed the night.

Next morning we walked the ten miles into Clear Lake, where they were setting up camp. When we got in there, we found a large group of 81 people, which made for a lively boisterous time. Charlie and Peggy Pierce, John and Betty Syverud, and Joe and Edith Stettner, friends from the Chicago Mountaineering Club were all there and Joe was the climbing leader, so we had a lot of really good climbs. The climbers built a sauna at the edge of the lake, by wrapping a large plastic covering over a frame and heating the inside with a fire on rocks. They would build up the fire and throw water on the rocks making steam and after sitting there for a period of time they would run out and jump into the lake. This was a great evening ritual after the tedious climbing of the day. It soon became so popular that they built a second one.

We had excellent weather the entire trip; only one out of the twelve days we were there was there any rain at all. The singing around the campfire started reluctantly each evening but gained both mellowness and variety as the night worn on. One night we waited until 1:30 for a party from Temple. Tired, hungry, but safe, they finally appeared.

Because this was a climbing outing, we started right away. I climbed Hay Stack (11,600 ft) with Charlie and Betty. It was a nice climb with a rappel off the backside. This mountain had a grass path clear to the top which Lenora climbed later. Next, I climbed East Temple (12,976 ft) which had more rock climbing than any other mountain on the outing. We next headed up Steeple (12,000 ft), another good rock climb. Jim Hagen had been in there the year before and had been forced off, so I let him lead the place they had turned back. We were soon on top and came back by the usual route on the back side.

Next on the agenda, Ollie and I climbed Temple (12,249 ft) by the west ridge. It has a high point, sometimes called West Temple. I climbed this with Ollie. It had a nice snow approach to the ridge with easy scrambling, and great views down the sides. We had to rappel down about sixty feet. The summit itself was a huge rock slab, with several cave-like formations. We took the snow down and picked up a rope that a previous party had left when it had become jammed during their rappel.

Meanwhile, Lenora took a hike with Joe and Edith which was a great experience, as the partners had climbed together so often they seemed to read the other's mind. When Edith got tired, she would say, "Slow down Seppi." Lenora uses the expression to this day when I go too fast.

The next day, Ollie asked me if I wanted to go to Lonesome Lake and climb War Bonnet. I jumped at the chance. We were going to climb the East Face, which was the route that Karl Bollinger fell from in 1953. There was Pat Armstrong, Britta Lingrem, Ollie and I and we camped below the face. From this angle, the mountain was spectacular as it was perpendicular with no visual handholds. This is the same mountain that I had climbed in 1953 and 1958 by a much easier route. We were going to climb the sheer east face. Ollie had been there the year before with Bill Primack and had established a new route, so this was the one we took. The fragile, thin north ridge went up for fifteen hundred feet. We roped up with Ollie and Britta on one line and I led Pat on the other. It began with a series of ledges, but soon turned into hard climbing. We came across two pitons placed there by Bollinger on his fatal climb. I pounded one out to take home in remembrance.

We finally were forced off the ridge to a traverse due to the lack of handholds. Here we combined the ropes, so the girls would have a belay from both ends because of the exposure. Ollie then left his pack, and then made a beautiful climb up a sloping slab, where he found a good belay position. As he tried to haul up his pack, his rope jammed. He needed another rope, so I had to untie mine and give it to him, so he could climb down and kick his pack loose. It was a very lonely feeling, clinging there like a fly on the wall, but I soon had a rope again and we went on to the top. This route is now called the Bollinger-Primack route and we got a second ascent. I have now climbed War Bonnet, three different ways. We returned down on the South face and went back to Clear Lake.

Next we drove over to the Tetons to see Orrin Bonney. While we were there, Orrin and I went down to see Barry Corbet give a talk on his climb of Everest. Barry recognized me from our days at Jenny Lake.

In the summer of 1966, Lenora and I found that we were expecting our first child, so instead of going to the mountains we went to Door County in

Wisconsin. We had a nice camp site in a state park. It was beautiful weather and our site had a nice beach. The area is very different than the mountains, but it had interesting towns, a lot like New England. We had a nice camp sites on the beach on Lake Michigan, all the towns had shops that we enjoyed.

Jacqueline was born in November and on News Years Day of 1967, we took her on our first New Year's Day Picnic at Lithia Spring on Lake Shelbyville. It was a beautiful sunny day, almost warm. The Park Service had just starting to put camp sites around where the lake was going to be and we had a nice picnic table. This became a family tradition that we have continued ever since—with Aunts, Uncles, In-laws, grandkids and family friends. Even today, forty years later, that outdoor picnic is special. It's often cold, sometimes snowy, sometimes clear and warm, but we always do it, and most years do a short hike together through the woods around Lake Shelbyville. It captures some of the spirit of those outings out west, the campfire and hot chocolate, some homemade stew or soup, and good friends sharing stories. It's just one of the small, but priceless, gifts that my climbing life bestowed upon me.

We met Charlie and Peggy Pierce at the Palisades in the spring. Charlie had a pack board to carry their three-month-old daughter Ann and I had five-month-old Jacque in a hike-a-pose. Peggy climbed Sentinel and gave us a belay, so we could climb up carrying the babies on our backs in their carriers. All the while, Lenora hid her eyes. It all turned out well, and we have pictures of the event. We probably have a record of the youngest ascents.

The next summer, 1967, we went to the Tetons and camped next to Jack and June in Coulter Bay. We took a lot of hikes with Jacque in a hike-a-poose on my back. We drove down to Jackson for shopping trips. Orrin Bonney now had a house in Kelly, Wyoming and we went there for supper one evening.

One day, we went down to Jackson and our car lost a wheel bearing. We limped the car over to the Ford Garage and they said it would be two days before they could get parts. While we were wondering what to do, we met some boys that were camped next to us, so we rode back to Coulter Bay with them. I hitchhiked back to Jackson the next day and retrieved the car. The missing part had come over from Salt Lake City on the bus.

We stayed home the next two years to welcome our daughter Allison and son Jonathan.

In 1970, we drove out to Estes and camped in a National Campground. By now we had a big mountain tent and found we could give baths in large bowls and eat together at the picnic tables. The camp site had about two inches of loose dirt on the floor and we found most of it found its way on the children before the day was over.

I took Jacque on my back up Flat Top Mountain through a lot of snow. She then finished the climb of Hallet's Peak (12, 713ft) on her own. It was a great pleasure to me to see her climbing at such an early age. After a day or two in the Campground, I took Allison up Chasm Lake for a picnic. We saw marmots and she called them puppy dogs. I took hikes with Jacque riding on my shoulders and Allison in the hike-a-poose. One time, we stopped to play in the stream and Allison slipped and fell into the stream, getting completely soaked. I pulled her out and took all of her clothes off and then divided Jacques clothes so each had ample covering to finish the hike.

It was three years before we got back to the mountains. In 1973, we went to Ouray, Colorado and camped in town at a private campground. There was a playground and things for the kids to play on which helped keep them happy. Friends from home camped next to us. One day Jacque and I took a tour up over the mountains to Telluride in an open jeep. This was as high as I got that year. I did take their boys up twin Oaks. They were about sixteen and this was their first mountain.

In 1977, we had a lot of snow in Illinois and we were snowbound several different times. One day, just to see if I could, I walked the six miles to town to work. Chill factor was thirty below zero, but since the wind came from the west, I didn't feel it. It fact I had to be careful I didn't get too warm.

In 1978, we took the family to California, and took in the Grand Canyon on the way, then drove on down to San Diego. While we were there we saw the Zoo, Sea World, and spent a lot of time on the beach. We did a side trip into Tijuana, Mexico, and ate lunch and looked over the town. Entering back into California, we were besieged by Mexicans, coming to our car, wanting to sell us their wares. We then drove up to Los Angeles, where we took in Hollywood, Universal Studios, Beverly Hills, and then up to San Francisco, to meet with Dudley and Mary Carter and their family. On the way, we had an accident that totaled the car. It was a Buick Station wagon, one of my all time favorite cars. We received a few scrapes and bruises, but other than that came out fine. We rented another car, and drove up to Sequoia National Park, and saw the giant redwoods. Dudley told us about a place to buy a car, so we bought a Chevrolet to drive the rest of the trip. In California, when you buy a car, you also buy the license plate, so we had the fun of driving home with California license. We saw Fisherman's Warf, China Town and the Golden Gate Bridge in San Francisco and then headed back to Illinois.

THE FAMILY

In 1979, when Jacque was twelve and I was fifty-one, I took her to Chicago Basin in Colorado with the Chicago Mountaineering Club on their western outing. We took the bus to Durango, which took a day and a half with stops at every town along the way.

We got up the first morning in Durango, carried our duffle over to the train station and took the Silverton train up to the Needleton Stop. It was a narrow gauge train, powered by steam with lots of coal smoke. We went through wooded hills and valleys where the average person never sees. Our car was full of climbers that were going on the outing. Jacque loved every minute and kept her head out of the window most of the way so she wouldn't miss anything.

When we came to our stop, we unloaded, crossed the bridge where the packer had set up a lunch stand. Groups began moving up the five and a half mile trail to the Chicago Basin base camp. Jacque tagged along with everyone, trying hard to keep up with the group. Our cooks had a delicious supper waiting of roast turkey with all the trimmings.

Our first climb was Jupiter which had a nice snow approach. Jacque did fine and we reached the peak about eleven in the morning. We had climbed up a snow gulley with snow so soft you couldn't fall if you tried.

I climbed Mount Aeolus the next day. Jacque stayed in camp and was really taken with the packhorses. At one point the leader used chocks for protection. This is the first time I had ever seen them used. Chocks are small pieces of metal in various shapes for placing in cracks, the carabineer (metal loop) hooks onto them and the rope passes through that. They are now the more popular alternative to pitons.

There was a big snowfield, and we stayed roped up. After crossing the snowfield, we found we were still not on top. About five hundred feet below, we untied and scrambled on up. After reaching what we thought was the top, the real summit was across the ridge, so we took another scramble and finally reached the summit. This mountain is 14,083 feet high and people were beginning to feel the altitude. On the way down, one man got so sick that he had to be rescued by horse.

The next day, Jacque and I took a hike up Columbine Pass through fields of the prettiest wildflowers I have ever seen. I took pictures of Jacque with flowers up to her waist. There were grouse along the trail so well camouflaged they seemed to appear out of thin air when they moved. We had lunch at the Pass. The packer had a good system. He had a table set up with bread, cold cuts, fruit, and candy and we then fixed our own lunch. There was a large variety of each and it made the lunches very nice.

Next, I climbed Windom, (14,082 ft) high. We had an unusual experience with electricity. One member of the party had her hair go straight up and the loose threads of her parka stood straight out. This happens a lot in the mountains. I assume the electricity in the air bounces off the rocks and acts like a magnet. The climb itself was just a walk up ledges after a steep snowfield. The snow was soft and easy to climb, but too soft to glissade down.

After another rest day, I climbed Sunlight. (14, 059ft) It was a nice rock climb that had a summit search, which I finally found. It was the best summit of the outing that came to a true point. Everyone had their picture taken, standing upright on the point. On the way down, a few of us decided to climb Peak 18. Staying as high as we could on the snow, leading to the saddle between Windom and Peak 18, there was a grassy ridge to the top and was a lot of fun. We made a quick trip down and arrived at the same time as the rest of the Sunlight party.

After a rest day, I decided to take Jacque up Aeolus, since it was a 14,000 foot mountain and the highest in the area. I had already climbed it, but I thought I knew a better way. We brought a couple other climbers with us. It was now nine o'clock, but since we had such a small party, we expected to make good time. It was mostly a snow climb to the saddle between Aeolus and North Aeolus. My friend Al led the way, kicking steps, with Jacque right behind him. I went behind her so we didn't need to rope. When we got to the rock, we left our ice axes and rope and scrambled up to the top. North Aeolus, 14,000 feet, was on a distant ridge, so we decided to go for it. It was a very enjoyable climb. Halfway over, I let Jacque take the lead. There was another party climbing on the other side and they were surprised to see an un-roped, twelve-year-old girl leading us. We came down to our ice axes and ropes, and began the long slide down. Jacque used her parka for a sled, so we got down very fast. We were in camp at five o'clock feeling good having climbed two fourteen'ers from "nine to five."

This was the last day in camp, so we had a giant campfire that night and awards were handed out. Jacque received the Pocahontas award for being the quietest climber in camp. I was given the reincarnation award, proving that Old Climbers Never Die. The next morning we hiked down to the railroad track and took the train to Durango. Norm Knox offered to take us back as far as Kansas City, so we rode that far with him. We then took a bus to Effingham where we met the rest of the family. Jacque kept a diary of all the food, and all the activities, so had many stories when we returned home.

In 1980, we took the whole family to Cape Hatteras. We got a nice campsite and spent a week on the ocean. We then drove up to Washington D.C. and visited all the historical sights. We went to Devil's Lake for Columbus Day and some of the climbers were disappointed we hadn't gone to the mountains that year.

The next year, it was Allison's turn to join me, but she didn't want to go to the mountains. So we took a canoe trip on the Current River in Missouri with a group of about thirty people. The Current is the Ozark Scenic River way and the water is so clear, we could see down about ten feet to the bottom, since it is fed by springs. The river twists and turns through tall cliffs, which made for beautiful scenery. We road the canoes until dark, camped on sand banks along the side of the river and had group cooking over open fires. It rained one day but that didn't bother us much.

In August of that year, the whole family went to the Tetons. Some friends were already there and saved us a campsite at Signal Mountain Campground. We took several hikes, among them Lake Solitude. At one point, we were up to our waists in bluebells, but the lake still had ice and there was still snow all around.

Allison and I went up Amphitheater Lake, and part way up Disappointment Peak. I tried to talk her up the rest of the way but she didn't want to go further. Funny to think that, thirty years later she climbed Kilimanjaro. We had some beautiful storms in camp that year, the lightning streaking in all directions across the sky.

I took Jonathan up Storm Point, which is a real mountain with a point on top. There were some good views of the mountains all around us. He was about ten years old, but it gave him a feeling of what mountain climbing was like and why I enjoy it so much.

After a rest day, Jacque and I started up the Grand. The Grand was an obvious choice, since it is so well known and well traveled, so we would always have help if we needed it. The disadvantage is that, it takes two days to climb, so I had to leave Lenora and the two kids below. It also meant carrying food and shelter for an overnight camp. We traveled very light, but I was still loaded down with thirty-five pounds (it is amazing how many meals there are in two days). We finally decided on a lot of breakfast bars and dried fruit. In those days, we could drink the water from the streams, so we didn't have to carry it. We got up to the meadows about two o'clock, had plenty of time to set up our camp. We used our tarp for a tent, by draping it between two boulders. We went to bed at dark, underneath the tarp that I had spread out, after a supper of granola bars and dried fruit. We woke up the next morning, hearing our neighbors cooking breakfast. Our breakfast was more granola bars and dried fruit, so it didn't take long to pack up and go.

I decided to go very slow, because we had a long way ahead of us. We would stop at the end of every switchback for a minute or two to rest. We saw the sun come up on Middle Teton; this was another example of Alpenglow. The sun hits the top turning it gold and finally works it way down until the whole mountain is gold. It was light by the time we got to the start of the climb, and there was already a lot of people ahead of us, so we decided to go on the Owen Spalding route since the Exum Ridge was crowded. I had never climbed this route, so I had trouble finding the way. After finding the route, I let Jacque go ahead of me, following right after her. We got to a place where there was a lot of exposure. The hard part of the climb was over, but the people with us were still nervous, so we roped up. There was a glider flying overhead circling the mountain, and the higher we got, the circle got closer to us, so we could tell we were getting closer to the top. We peaked and signed the register at about three in the afternoon. We then made our way down to the rappel point. It was about a hundred-foot rappel and I went first to be on the bottom to take pictures. We had made friends with some climbers and they made certain Jacque was secured and tied in properly. She made the rappel fine and I got some real good pictures. After the rappel, it is just a long hard trek down to our campsite. We packed up and started down the trail. By now, it was dark, and we didn't get down to the parking lot where Lenora, Allison, and Jonathan were waiting until ten that night. They were lying on their backs watching the falling stars.

The next day, we started home via Yellowstone National Park. We stayed in a cabin that night and visited some of the sights, then continued home.

The next year, we returned to Cape Hatteras, and stayed in the private campground that we had stayed in the time before. The only thing we climbed that year were the sand dunes at Kill Devil Hills. We saw the place the Wright Brothers flew their plane and a replica of the plane. We spent most of the time on the beach, feeding the sea gulls, and making sand castles.

In 1983, Jonathan and I went to Jean Lake in the Wind Rivers in Wyoming. We drove to Route 80, south of Chicago, to pick up a friend. Then we drove on through to Pinedale, Wyoming, where we took a forest service road to Freemont Lake and left our car at the trailhead. There was a long hard walk in, but the Chicago Mountaineer Club had set up a nice campsite. This was the first time we had to take our own food, but we were allowed fifty pounds each for the packers to take in for us. We set up our own little cooking area, and made a neat campsite.

The first day we went out on a huge snowfield, so Jonathan could try out his crampons. I had adjusted some I had to fit his boots. We were glad there was a lot of snow, because it made it seem like we were really in the mountains. I had planned for enough meals to last ten days and it was really fun to get started cooking. The second day we climbed a rock formation called The Knob. We had to cross the creek to get to it, and it was amazing how much bigger the stream got by evening. The snow melts upstream during the day and we had watched carefully that we didn't get stranded.

We joined a large group the next day to climb a mountain called Stroude (12,200 ft). After a snow approach, we climbed up the East Ridge for a very easy climb to the summit. The view was fantastic, since there was so much snow. We could see Gannet with Mammoth Glacier flowing down its side and the valley where the Green River started. This was July 23rd, my wedding anniversary, so everyone wished me a happy anniversary. It was late when we got down, so we decided we wouldn't climb anything the next day.

Several of us got together and cooked a noon meal with different foods for about ten people. We had several stoves that we sat on rocks, so people could just dip into whatever pot they wanted. One person even cooked pancakes for everyone, which we ate like bread. It felt very primitive, but made it memorable. In the evenings, after supper, Jon and I would retire to our tent, where we had a candle lantern that I had made from a 7UP can, and soon were asleep, hoping to remember to blow out the candle.

The next mountain we climbed was G17 (11, 900 ft), by the snow approach. I took Jonathan, and two others and we started up on a cloudy day. As soon as we got to the snow, we put on our crampons. About halfway up it began to snow, so we looked for a place to wait it out. After about an hour, it stopped so we began climbing again. We were on a nice easy ridge, so I let Jonathan go on ahead, and he got to the top by himself. We got a good view of Henderson from the top with its black and white south face. We started down and were soon on snow again, so we tried to glissade, but the snow was too soft, so we ended up just running down. We got down by three o'clock.

Arrowhead (12,600ft) was the mountain everyone wanted to climb, so we decided to do it next. Jonathan, Pieter Fockens and I left about seven o'clock and made good time. We had crampons, but decided to go up without them because the snow was so soft. Sometimes snow can pack up in the spikes and cause accidents.

We bypassed the little frozen lake and were soon on the col (saddle) between Arrowhead and Buchtel. After going up a steep snowfield, we left our ice axes and went straight up through rocks, with easy scrambling. I again let Jonathan go ahead and he reached the top about noon. It was a glorious day. We had lunch and just looked and looked. We took pictures in all directions and then looked some more. We could see the Tetons with the Grand and Mount Moran clearly visible. To the south, we could see Mount Temple in the Southern Wind Rivers. But close in, the view was just as good. We could see Gannet, Woodrow Wilson, Helen, and Freemont. I've asked Jonathan if he would be able to describe this to his mother, and he said "No. How can I?" Peter Fockens said it best, "Just remember your finest experience on a mountain top, that's what it was like for us." We finally had to leave hoping we could retain this memory. On the way down, we went through a forest of Colorado Blue Spruce of mixed sizes from thirty feet to two feet tall, all shaped like perfect Christmas trees.

John Harkness decided to try to climb Mount Henderson, so I signed up with him. Henderson (named after Ken Henderson, who climbed most of these mountains in the 1930s) is a mountain far off the beaten path. To reach it, we had to go clear around G17, past frozen lakes, where we got our first good view of the peak. The guidebook said to go up the ridge, but John thought it would be more fun to go up the south face. This was the same face I had seen while we were waiting out the snowstorm on G17. After the end of the snowfield, the rocks started and we roped up. We had two ropes and we headed up parallel over easy terrain. I was roped with Carol Karps and we swapped leads, looking for the summit. We went up three different peaks before we found the right one. Carol and I were on the first rope to the summit. When we found the register, it was the original one, with Ken Henderson's recorded first ascent, forty years earlier. We read through eleven other entries, and realized we were the only ones that had climbed the peak from the South. So we decided we had the first ascent by that route. Now we had the long way down, but were able to rappel part way. It was nine o'clock before we got back, but we had accomplished a lot.

They had arranged for packers to come and get our camping gear, so we had to leave the outing early. We thought about driving over to the Tetons for a couple of days, but when I called home, I found out my father was very ill and about to die. We drove home and got there in time for the funeral.

KEEPING THE TRADITION ALIVE

In 1993, we took the family up to Devil's Lake on Memorial Day, for my fortieth anniversary of climbing with the CMC Club. I took thirty bottles of Champagne and we finished most of them. There were about sixty people there and everyone had a good time.

In 1996, Allison's husband Steve and I went to Rocky Mountain National Park, where Jack Gorby was having a small outing. We camped at Olive Ridge campground. It was a National Forest Campground, really clean and very enjoyable. Jack Gorby had a cabin about a mile away, and some of the climbers camped in his backyard.

We had a snowstorm one night and my tent fell in on me. Next day, I shook the snow off and straightened the poles, and it was as good as new. Estes Park was about ten miles north, so we drove there to eat, wash clothes and take showers. The elk had come down from the mountains and were just walking around the town. The townspeople thought nothing of it.

There was a lot of snow, so we mostly took hikes. One day, we climbed Flat Top (12,324 ft) in a blizzard where the snow was as high as our knees. We tried to climb in someone else's footprints, which is called post holing. It was snowing so hard on top that we actually thought maybe we had climbed Hallets, the mountain next to Flat Top. After it cleared up in a day or two, we discovered we had climbed an outcropping of Flat Top. It is surprising how you lose track of every thing in a blizzard. The next day, we all went up Twin Sisters, through more deep snow. I fell behind, but enjoyed the solitary hike. They were waiting for me on top, and we enjoyed about an hour up there. We had a farewell dinner in Estes.

Steve, Jonathan and I went to Devil's Lake that fall with the CMC. When we got there, there was snow on the ground. We set up our camp anyway.

Next day, Ollie Swartling led a party to the sandstone area of the park. I was climbing an easy practice pitch, when I slipped and fell about ten feet. Instead of stopping at the bottom of the climb, I slid on some leaves until I stopped, hitting my ankle on a rock. I didn't think much about it, and we went on climbing the rest of the day. I didn't do any more climbing and just belayed the two boys. I limped back to the car, now beginning to wonder if there was anything wrong with my ankle. I could move it all direction, wiggle my toes, so I thought it must be just a bruise. I went to work Monday, hobbling around, still thinking it just a bruise. I finally went to the Doctor and got an x-ray and they found out the tibia bone (the one that sticks out on the ankle) was broken and would need surgery. I went to the Hospital and they attached it with a pin. I never did have to stop work. Ollie was writing a new guidebook and as a joke called this climb: Broken Foot.

In the spring of 1997, Jonathan and I went back to Rocky Mountain National Park and Olive Ridge, where Jack Gorby was holding an outing. Charlie Pierce came out and joined us. The first day we took a hike around Twin Owls, and I was able to point out practice climbs that we had done in the fifties. Jonathan and I climbed Estes Cone, and I was surprised what a nice climb it was. The next day, Jack got up a party to go to Twin Sisters. It was hard to believe the difference since there was no snow. We got a great view of the east face of Long's Peak from the top of Twin Sisters. From that distance, we could see the magnitude of the face. It looked like someone had taken a giant cleaver and sliced off part of the mountain leaving the face exposed. Jack Gorby took us up to a snow field and conducted a school that was very educational. I had rented some snow shoes, and learned how to walk in them.

One of the founders of the CMC, Jack Fralik, was going to be in Boulder so we all went down to have dinner with him. This was the first time I had met him, but we knew each other by reputation. The man had climbed everywhere. We struck up a friendship, that I continued the rest of his life. I called him, every couple of months with climbing news. We spent our trip home reliving our good memories.

GO EAST

That fall, Lenora and I went to Japan, to visit Steve and Allison, who were teaching English. We saw many wonderful sights, the temples, wonderful gardens, and Tokyo at night with all of the lights. The Kanto region rests a range of mountains called Tanzawa, where there is a popular two-day hike, with four peaks to enjoy. We took a train to a village called Shibusawa and there we picked up a bus to Okura. The start of the trail was a short walk to a well-trodden path, where there were many other hikers. I was accustomed to the switchbacks of American mountains but here the trail headed straight up with wooden steps installed in the steepest areas.

We arrived at Tonodake peak first, where there were wooden picnic benches and good views of Mount Fuji. This mountain is the one you associate with Japan. It is a perfect triangle with a snow covered top. Everyone in Japan wants to climb it at least once. Next we hiked through a forest of bamboo; it was interesting to see that many "fishing poles." There were many azalea bushes, but because it was fall, they were not in bloom. We soon came to the summit of Tanzawayama, but the forest didn't yield good views. After that, the trail dropped down steeply and then climbed to a ridge with drop offs on both sides. From this point, we could see Fuji clearly. Then the trail leads to the summit of Hirugatake and here we found a hut in which to stay overnight. We ate dinner and Steve stayed up practicing his Japanese. I was so tired, I went right to bed.

The next morning, they served us breakfast. There was no water source for our canteens but the staff told us of a spring on the way down. There was a long east ridge walk to Yakeyama, but we decided to pass and started down. We never did find the spring and I was really hurting for water. The trail goes straight down to the village of Nagano, with thatched-roof cottages, and vegetable plots. By this time, I was completely dehydrated and lost all strength in my legs. When I tried to sit on a bench, I would just fall so we kept walking. I forced my legs onward like a zombie. When we finally got to the village, I bought a diet Coke and felt better almost at once.

We took the bus back to the train station and then arrived back to the apartment. The next day I was so stiff, I could hardly walk down steps. This was a wake up call, as we were planning to go to Nepal in February.

In 1997, Allison and Steve went to Nepal and did a trek. They journeyed from Phaplu to Tengpoche and were so impressed that they wanted me to join them the next year. After climbing with Steve in Japan, I knew I would need to train hard. I began riding a stationary bicycle and using a stair stepper for 1/2 hour every other night. I was still working ten hours, so was exhausted by the end of the day.

After a lot of planning, we finally were ready to go in February of 1998. Allison and Steve held a farewell party with a lot of banners and music. We stopped in Champaign-Urbana and had supper with my son Jon, who was still in college. Steve suddenly remembered he left his boots, so he had to drive the sixty miles back to get them while we waited in the restaurant. We then drove on to Chicago, where we would stay over night with Steve's family.

The next morning we boarded our flight at O'Hara and landed in Tokyo twelve hours later. After a three-hour lay over, it was on to Bangkok, where we stayed at a Comfort Inn. The next morning we had an exotic breakfast (included in the price just as it is in the American chain), with lots of new things to try, such as fresh mangoes and papaya.

The airport in Bangkok was fascinating, with so many Far East lines I had never heard of before. We took off at 10:00 a.m. on a Royal Nepal Airline plane and followed the coastline all the way to India. Below us there were rivers and forests, but very few roads. Eventually villages began to appear on a huge delta—Bangladesh.

When mountains of Nepal came into view, all of us scooted to the windows and tried to locate Everest, but couldn't be sure which it was. Nonetheless, it was a calendar view, with clouds floating below the peaks. As we descended, we began to discern little terraced settlements, just like in *National Geographic.* We approached a lush, green valley and landed in Katmandu at 1:30 p.m. Nepal time, which is exactly twelve hours and fifteen minutes ahead of CDT. We were halfway around the globe from home.

We had to buy a Visa before we could leave the airport and were faced with a throng of men clamoring for us to stay at their guesthouse. Since we were headed for Thamel we picked one in that section of the city. It turned out to be a bad choice, as it was too rustic—even for us. I had to work on the toilet to get it to flush. There were even broken windows in the room. After checking in, we walked to the center of Thamel for supper and sight seeing. We ate at Northfield Cafe, and had very good food. It seemed like mushrooms were in most every dish. We made arrangements for a taxi to pick us up at 4: 30 in the morning, to take us up to Nagarot to see the sunrise. Steve and Allison had done this the year before and said it was a must see.

We had car trouble but we were soon picked up by another cab and continued on. It was cloudy, unfortunately. I was more impressed with the ride up, as the city was just waking, with the farmers bringing their produce to market. They had all sorts of hand-drawn wagons. There were so many colors—reds, blue, yellows with so many sounds of people with carts, monkeys, birds, and the banging of those setting up stands. As we started up the side of the hill, it came alive with lights, one at a time—very spectacular! On the way down, all the villagers were working, even the small children. It reminded us of the Amish.

We got returned in time for breakfast at the Northfield. It was very nice weather and we ate omelets and mint tea outside in their garden. I bought a *USA Today* newspaper and was really impressed that it was only one day old.

We chose a new guesthouse called Newars that we liked a lot better and it reminded me of those I had stayed at in Quebec. It was a no frills, but small, very clean room—smaller than motel rooms in the States. It is right in the atmospheric heart of Thamel. I stood outside waiting on Steve and Allison and just took everything in. There was every kind of transportation: small cars honking their horns, motor scooters, rickshaws, bicycles, golf carts and more. There were carts of fruits and vegetables passing by and men playing small violins to sell them. The maid of our hotel was sweeping the sidewalk with a small fireplace-style broom and it seemed a losing battle. It was very dusty and I soon developed a cough which stayed with me the rest of the trip. The air was musty and filled with the scents of food cooking, as every other building was a restaurant. There was every culture of cuisine: German, Chinese, Italian, and of course, Kentucky Fried Chicken and McDonald's.

To see the rest of the city, we took a small cart to Freak Street where I bought a pair of trekking poles. It was once a haven for hippies in the sixties, but they have since eliminated most of the drug dealers. We ate at a rooftop restaurant overlooking a flea market and then walked back to our guesthouse through every kind of market you could imagine. There would be a spice market, then a fruit market, then a hardware market, then clothing, then bookstores, all outside. We stopped at a bank to change our money and get small bills as the guidebooks tell us, so it ended us with a stack of bills about three inches thick. We also got our trekking permit and checked in at the American Embassy. This was the first time I had ever even been in one. It reminded me of our post offices.

We then packed up for our Trek and left what we didn't need at the hotel for safe keeping in a special room that they have for this purpose. We had to get up at five to catch our flight to Lukla. This would cut off a week from our trek, because we were trying to get to Everest base camp or Kalla Patar. We waited in the lobby while flight controllers watched the weather and decided whether or not to fly. The room was filled with very interesting people—lots of families trying to go home and trekkers trying to go to Lukla. About 9:00 o'clock, they cancelled, but said we could go on the helicopter, since we already had a ticket.

The helicopter was a big Russian cargo carrier, filled with freight in the center and benches for about twenty passengers along the hull. After we got seated, the pilot passed out cotton for our ears and chewing gum to help them equalize. We took off about 9:30 a.m. and flew low to stay out of the clouds. We could see hundreds of small, hillside villages from our window. It seemed every square foot was terraced farmland.

Around 10:45 we arrived in Lukla, a town about a half mile long with lodges on both sides of the trail. The landing field was crowded with men trying to get work as guides or offering their lodge. Because Allison and Steve had been there the previous year, they knew where to stay. Our lodge was called Panorama. We got a room with a double bed and a small bed for me. There was a small dining room with large wooden tables. We ate Sherpa Stew for lunch, consisting of broccoli, cabbage, carrots, and onions served with tea and brown sugar. It was cold, but I had enough clothes to keep warm. My new sleeping bag is light but warms up quick.

We woke around 5:30 and went down to the airstrip to watch the sun come up. The bright orange starts at the top and works its way down much like the Aspen Glow in the mountains at home. But since it was on a snow covered mountain, it was more spectacular.

After breakfast, we hired a young man named Jom Boy to carry our extra clothing and sleeping bags. We would each carry up to twenty pounds and he would carry forty. In addition to our gear, Jom Boy carried a huge cheese round to deliver to a teahouse on the trail. Steve had planned the route and the towns we would stop in and Jom Boy would find us a teahouse and show us the way. We agreed to pay him ten dollars each day.

It was a clear day and we wanted to stay and see the plane land but decided to get started on our trek. The trail was almost as wide as a single lane road and level for the first five miles. We began to see yaks, with bells on, so you could hear them coming from a long way off. Some were caring loads, but most were just going up the trail. Because it was spring, we assumed they were going up to pasture.

We passed waterfalls and traversed at least three swinging bridges. To give you an idea of the weather, I was wearing a light undershirt with no hat.

We stopped to eat lunch at the teahouse, where we would be spending the night. The dining room was small with a wood stove in the middle. None of the furniture matched as if it had been gathered up a piece at a time over the years. It took about an hour to get our food, but it was very good: potatoes with cabbage and onions all fried together. I went to bed about 5:30 because there wasn't anything else to do. I had to get up in the middle of the night to go outside and the stars were beautiful.

We awoke at seven. The dining room had dried fruits and nuts in wooden bowls on each table. It was Sherpa New Year (they have a different calendar), so that had to be our breakfast. Looking out the window, we could see mountains with no names that were prettier than any I had ever seen. We were so high and the mountains were so huge, that the view in every direction was breathtaking. Around us, there were little garden plots with cabbages ready to pick, each plot enclosed with a rock walls. There were many porters tramping by on the trail. A guest at the Lodge had been on a trek to Tengpoche and he told me, your knees get sore on the way down. He gave me two braces to wear with the stipulation that I give them to someone else when I got down.

We met up with a Japanese man that was climbing alone. Steve and Allison started to talk to him to practice their Japanese, so he started traveling with us. He went the whole trek. He was a very good traveling companion and he always paid more than his share and stayed in the same room with Ed.

Namchee Bazaar was our next stop. I was surprised how wide the trail was and there was no sense of danger at all. I had to rest a lot, but I would recover fast. There were quite a few people on the trail; no one was going faster than we were. There was a stop along the way where you can see Everest for the first time. Everywhere you look, it is a calendar view. We got to the town and had lunch and then explored the town, the largest on our trek.

The lodge there was called Khunba, owned by the sister of the lodge owner in Lukla. Jom Boy delivered the cheese here. The owner was a dentist that had gone to Canada to get her education, and then came back to practice in Nepal. Her husband had been a Sherpa on Everest nine times. We talked to him a lot, and he told us to drink at least a gallon of water and to rest at least 2 days on the way. We would stay here one day. The lodge served very good meals with potatoes and rice, with cheese or mushroom soup. Everyone gathered in the large dining room, so we met some very interesting people. There was a young couple who were climbing guides in Washington State. I can remember a time when that would appeal to me, but I was so glad that I didn't choose that way of life.

The next day I woke up at seven for breakfast, which consisted of Tibetan bread with a big pot of tea. The bread was the size of your plate with butter and syrup and was very good. After breakfast, we went to the Bazaar because this was the day they held it. People came from miles around to buy and sell. A real social event. They had everything you can imagine to sell, even raw meat. They drive water buffalo there, then butcher them and sell the meat. I bought a necklace for my granddaughter, Adriene. Each vendor had a handheld calculator and when you asked the price, they typed it in and handed you the calculator with the price on it. If you wanted to haggle, you wrote your offer and it went back and forth until you both agreed.

That afternoon, I took a walk around the city, while Allison and Steve hiked up the side of the mountain behind of the village. Namchee is a crossroad with trails going in all directions, clear to Tibet. There were over a hundred hotels during our stay; there may be twice that number now. That evening, we talked to our porter about carrying my pack. I felt I would enjoy my trip much more that way. We went to bed about 8:30 and I slept pretty well, but when you drink that much water, you have to get up a lot. The toilets were seat-less, generally just a hole in the floor with a bowl of water to wash yourself with. Everyone carried a towel to dry themselves with.

The dining room had a lot of new faces for breakfast with everyone telling where they had been and their future plans. As far as I was concerned, this trek would be my biggest and I felt lucky to be doing it. My porter started calling me Papa, so everyone else did too. I even began to sign my meal tickets that way.

Our next stop was the entrance to Sagarmatha National Park, where our permits were checked. And then again at Khumjuny, which is a small village with two or three lodges. Ours lodge was called Ama Dablam, a mountain on the horizon. We could also see Everest from here. We arrived early in the afternoon and had a good lunch in an outdoor dining area. It reminded me of 1989, when we first got to Austria and ate outside, even though it is cold, when you are that high, the sun feels warmer. We relaxed while our porter brought us up some hot lemonade, which I now preferred to tea. I ordered boiled potatoes with mushroom soup. When it arrived, there were about ten potatoes in all.

Steve and Allison took a short hike, but I stayed in my room. I could hear the yak bells in the distance, growing in volume until they passed by my room. I'll never forget it. I thought of home and how glad I was that Lenora wanted me to make this trip. One of our traveling companions said, "Some views are so big your camera can't capture them, but these views are too big for your eyes to capture!" After supper, we sat in the dinning room by ourselves and watched two women assemble a long line of prayer flags. They sewed the flags onto a rope. It was very colorful. I woke up in the night and went outside. The stars were so bright and seemed close because the air is thin and there are few city lights.

The next morning, I woke up at six, went outside to watch the sunrise and decided the view from my window was just as good. For breakfast, I had scrambled eggs for the first time in weeks. They bring the eggs by yak in big crates and you wonder how many get broken on the trip up.

We left at nine and it was a short, but steep trail to Tengpoche. We walked on through the town because the porter knew of a better place to stay. It was a new lodge with fresh stain on the walls. Though it was typically a ten-minute walk, it was very icy and took about thirty minutes. After checking in, we went back to Tengpoche, which is widely thought to be the most beautiful place in the world. We could see eight mountains over 20,000 feet high. They have a very pretty monastery with a long tradition. It was first built in 1919, and then destroyed by an earthquake in 1934. After being rebuilt, it burned in 1984. The latest was built in 1993, with a lot of international help. We took a tour of it and it was very interesting. The monks were at study and there were a lot of paintings and religious items. This was as far as Allison and Steve had gotten the year before so I was thankful I had made it that far.

We went back to our lodge for a pot of hot lemonade and supper of rice with curry pea soup. We interrupted our meal to see the sunset over Everest and Ama Dablin and got some very good pictures, but of course, they couldn't do it justice. After supper, our porters came around and tried to communicate. We liked them a lot. Jom Boy only knew two words of English. Every time we asked him, "How much farther?" he said, "Half hour."

It was very cold at night and my new sleeping bag felt good. The hike the next morning was nice. It was along the river and not too steep. Everest loomed all along the way. We stopped for lunch at Shomore (13, 000 ft), crossed another swinging bridge. This was one of the most exciting things about our trek. There were handrails of course, but we were up about 1000 feet above the gulley! We had to time our steps, to keep the bridge from swinging too much.

We stopped at Dingboche for two days to rest up. This lodge was the best one yet. We even had showers with water heated by the sun. We had a big sunroom and the sun was out full force. It heated the room very well at this altitude. We met a couple from Champaign, who taught at the University of Illinois. They were familiar with the area where I was raised, Lake Shelbyville and the Amish Community. After supper, one of our porters tried to play the harmonica. It sounded more like bagpipes but we were honored.

After breakfast, we hiked the hill behind our lodge. You are supposed to go up high and then come down on your days off to acclimate. Allison climbed for about two hours, but Steve went on up for another hour, while I waited and could see Island Peak and Makalu in the distance. Island Peak is possible to climb without a lot of backup for the average person. It is about 20,000 feet, and has a very easy approach. It looks like a giant snow cone on a large snowfield. Dingboche has a lot of summer pastures and there was one outside our window. We watched the owner gather dung after the yaks were in the shed to use for fire fuel. The names of all the lodges and their menus were in English. Our lodge was called Solar Friendship Lodge & Restaurant. It was the best place we stayed, the owners had some outdoor lawn chairs brought up on yaks and they were very proud of them. We met an English couple for supper that had traveled around the world. We talked with them until the lights went out. Because most things were solar powered, festivities shut down about 8:30 pm.

When we got up for breakfast, the owners were still in bed (they slept in the dinning room). We watched as they donned layer upon layer of clothing. They told us they had been to the United States and had traveled all over the West.

It turned cloudy for the first time, and it seemed as we trekked higher it would stay that way. We climbed the same hill that we had climbed the day before and then we hit the trail. It started to snow and I say in my notes that "It wasn't fun anymore. There is no view a hundred yards ahead." We did have a very good lunch in a little shanty in Duglha, so we felt good for a while. The trail started up for about a mile, and just when I felt I couldn't go any further, it leveled off. We passed a row of stone monuments in memory of Sherpas and climbers that had died on Everest. We didn't count them, but the guidebook said eighteen or more. It began snowing very hard, and we wondered if we would he able to climb the next day. We had to cross a long snowfield where we couldn't see the bottom. There had been yaks along the trail, so it was packed very hard.

We finally got to Lobuje about three in the afternoon. The lodge was the most rustic so far—essentially stalls instead of rooms, about four feet by eight feet, without heat. We talked to a man that had just climbed Kafla Patar that day, and he didn't think it was worth climbing. He said he couldn't see because of the snow and the climbing was very hard. We decided that unless it cleared off we wouldn't try it. In 1996, there was a huge snowstorm and people were stuck here for about a week. That was in the last of March, so we knew it could happen to us. We had a very nice supper of boiled potatoes and mushroom soup. We stayed in the dining room because it was the warmest place. There was a stove in the middle of the room and the young owner would burn dung, a little at a time. He and his wife had a one-year-old and seemed very happy. In the middle of the night I had to go outside and it was clear. I didn't know if I was glad about this or not, because if it was clear the next morning, we would continue the climb. When I got back in bed, I wore everything I had and even used my coat for a blanket.

The next morning, it was snowing again, so we decided to start back down the mountain. We each found a small rock to bring back to mark the highest point of 16, 000 feet. We took pictures of the lodge and the owners and their baby. I was very sorry to start back, but as it turned out, it snowed all that day, so it was the right decision. As we came to the snowfield, I was nervous because I didn't know if the trail would still be there, but it was okay. We were at 16, 000 feet with temperature around ten degrees. I was wearing all the clothes I had brought with me with visibility of five or six feet. We stopped for lunch at Pheriche at a nice teahouse. It was still snowing and as we looked back, we could see nothing but snow. After lunch, we had to climb a little and I didn't think I could make it. We stopped and I put on one of Allison's sweaters and then we went on. I started to feel a lot better and the trail leveled off, so we decided to go clear to Debouche and stay at the same lodge that we had stayed in on the way up. It had even stopped snowing about four o'clock. It was amazing how much difference it made. I started to feel great since we were losing altitude.

While we were eating, a Japanese man became sick with AMS (when your blood gets so thick it collects in the brain and lungs). He got so bad, one of his friends and the lodge owner took him down to the next village about 1500 feet below. When they returned they said he was doing fine. Apparently if you get to lower altitude quick enough you'll recover. We were told to drink lots of water, and of course we did and stayed well.

As we started, Everest and Ama Dablam were in clear view. For the next hour we remained in Tengpohe, savoring the most magnificent view in the world. We were lucky that there were no clouds. The trail takes a big drop and then rises back up to Namchee Bazaar. We stayed at the Khumbu Lodge again and I treated myself to a yak steak. You can tell if someone orders a steak, because you can hear the pounding from the kitchen. Some people ordered Monos which is vegetables rolled in mashed potatoes and then deep fried. It looked awfully good. I was feeling great, even though 1'd gotten tired on the trail. After a few minutes rest, I was good to go again.

On the last day of our trek, we passed many rhododendrons, but they hadn't bloomed yet. There were many prayer rocks along the way, huge boulders carved with prayers on them. You are to walk around the left side of it, so your left hand is away from the rock. In Nepal, the left hand is considered unclean.

We arrived in Lukla about six o'clock and stayed in the same lodge that we stayed in on the way up. We were worried that we couldn't get a plane ride out because we were early, but the owner of the lodge arranged for us to ride on the helicopter. We were very lucky because occasionally people get stuck in Lukla for days.

During supper, a Tibetan sold rugs and jewelry. Steve bought a rug. I bought a stainless steel plate. I gave our porter my wool shirt. We had gotten to really like him and knew we would never see him again. The next morning he came to the airport to tell us good-bye.

The ride back to Kathmandu was better than the way up because the sun was out and we could see a lot more. We got back to our hotel and checked in and reclaimed our luggage. By now, we felt we knew our way around. We ate our lunch outside at the Northside and bought another *USA Today* for the latest news. Again, it was just one day old. After lunch, we went shopping for gifts. Allison recognized the owner of the sweater shop from the previous year. I purchased sweaters made from yak yarn for gifts to take home. We took showers for the first time in days and then went out for a good meal at a fancy Thai restaurant. Allison bought a tape of the music they were playing.

The next morning, I rose early and went up on the roof to look out over the city. For the rest of my life I will recall those neighboring roofs with their little gardens. Kathmandu isn't that far north, so many plants grow year-round. On the streets below, there were children walking to school with their uniforms on. I believe these were from more affluent families because there were still many young kids running around in the middle of the day. An old lady was trying to sweep the sidewalk, again with a small hearth-style broom. As I looked closer, I could see she had a child on her back with her garment flipped over its head.

We had breakfast at the Northside in the garden again. It was really warm and it felt good in the shade. I still had my cough, it seems like this is a common ailment because of the dust in the air. The town had come to life and there was turmoil in the street with all the different modes of transportation. All the taxis honked their horns, every ten seconds.

There is a trekking company and outdoor supply store and I bought a bigger duffel bag so I could bring our yak wool sweaters home. We saw many young men in Nehru suits with Indian caps, all carrying briefcases—on their way up in the business world.

We decided on a trip to Bhaktapur, which is a village about 20 miles away. The countryside was very interesting with small farms. There were a lot of brick houses, so I think brick must be cheap. We took a taxi and as we arrived, young men screamed to be our guide. We told them we didn't want any, but one kept at our side the whole tour. Dunbar Square is a large area with dozens of temples and other old buildings. There were no cars, so you walk through narrow streets to one large open space after another. It is unbelievable, so we took pictures.

Next, we went to Patan, a suburb of Katmandu, with huge courtyards of temples, like the ones in Bhaktapur. It was a lot cleaner with a lot of hand-carved walls. There were big thick gates at the entrance to the courtyards. I bought Adriene a small box of handmade dolls.

We then went to Swayam Hunath, the most popular shrine in Nepal. We took a van to the bottom of the hill and then walked on a steep incline to the top. The temple has a big dome with prayer wheels all around the outside. It was the most spectacular thing in Kathmandu. There were prayer flags hanging from the top tier, where monkeys were crawling. Both Hindus and Buddhists believe the shrine spontaneously emerged from a lakebed.

That night we ate at a really fancy restaurant. You had to take off your shoes at the door and sit cross-legged on the floor. There were long, low tables scattered throughout the room and the food was so different than the stews we had been eating. Many different kinds of meat fixed like a stir fry which was a welcome change.There is only cooked food in this area as fresh produce is likely to make one sick. My meal cost three dollars.

Since we got down from our trek so early, we decided to take a two-day trip to Pokhara. This is where all the treks to Annapurna start. We went to the Kathmandu Guest House and arranged for a taxi. He agreed to take us there, stay for two nights and then bring us back for twenty dollars.

The ride over was great. We followed a river most of the way, with swinging bridges for people to cross over to get to their homes. The people are very poor and many of the children work. There are a lot of big trucks with highly decorated boards on the top of the cab like circus wagons. We don't know why, maybe each is trying to out do the other. We saw farmers starting to plant their spring crops on terraced hills. They used two cattle to pull a big plow. Closer to Pokhara, the climate became almost Floridian. We saw trees with little bananas growing. We stopped at a teahouse for lunch. Our table was in a little garden with tropical flowers. All of the bigger villages have things for sale along the side of the road. They had the little stringed instruments like we saw Thramel.

We found a nice hotel for about four dollars a night. It had tiled floors with polished woodwork. It's what I picture South Africa might look like, with flowers everywhere, even the coffee bushes. There was a big lake called Phewa Tal. We ate supper by the water's edge and stayed all evening until the full moon came up.

The next morning, we walked back to the center of the town to eat breakfast. We were disappointed that it was cloudy so we couldn't see the mountains and that was the main reason we came here. We took a hike down to a place they call Devils Hole, where the river goes underground. They were having a holiday called Hoh, where everyone throws red powder over you; even the little kids have their sacks. It only happens one day a year.

Steve and Allison went to a fancy place for supper, but I wasn't feeling very well, so I just went up on the roof of our hotel and watched the sunset. Red and yellow clouds parted over the blue sky to reveal Annapurna. I sat there until it was completely dark and the snow-covered mountains glowed in the moonlight.

We ate breakfast at our lodge, the Garden Guest Hotel. There was an older woman staying there too and I wondered what her story was. I went to the roof again to get my last took at the mountains. Besides Annapurna, there was Machhapuchhare with its fish-tailed peak. The natives believe the mountain is holy and thus it has never been climbed. Annapurna is about thirty miles from town and Machhapuchhare is about twenty, which makes for a beautiful panoramic view. There was a lot of new snow, so all those clouds the day before dumped their load here.

We left about ten o'clock for a five-hour drive. I was still amazed at the poverty. The women were gathering leaves in huge blankets to feed their cattle and goats. Cows and water buffalo stood around everywhere, their owners unknown.

The land flattened out and reminded us of heading down the South St. Vriam in Colorado. There was a lot of terrace farming with roadside stands selling produce. About every two or three miles would be a water pipe coming out of the side of the hill, sometimes mothers bathing their small children. We went through an area where they were breaking up rocks by hand. Even the little kids had hammers. I guess it was all part of growing up in this region. The Kathmandu Valley was very lush with many brick homes. Almost all of the houses look like they are only half-built, with the corner post going up for a second story.

After checking our tickets, we found we had another day so we decided to go to Boudhawath. This was the Hindu section about seven miles from Kathmandu. They boast the biggest Hindu Temple in the world. It is a giant sphere with a tower and prayer flags hanging. It is almost as big as an American small-town square, with little shops on the outskirts. We were not allowed in, but looked in through a big gate. We took many pictures, but they don't convey how big the temple was.

Next, we climbed up a small hill with crowds sitting or standing alongside the walk. Since it was Hindu area, the crowd looked very different—long hair, body piercing, sitting cross-legged, even some snake charmers. You could look across the river and see where they cremate the bodies. After they burn them, they push the ashes into the river. They have an assembly line and do this all day long. The Bagmato River flows into the Ganges.

We had our last dinner at a German Restaurant and said our goodbyes to our Japanese friend.

The hotel we stayed in Kathmandu was called Nemar. It had five floors with five rooms on each floor. We liked the boy that ran the place a lot and he let us leave our luggage in a storage room and he also did our laundry. We left most of our luggage when we went to Pokhara, so he was a good friend. We went to Dunbar Square for lunch on our last day and ate good pizza on the roof. We watch the flea market below or the monkeys on surrounding roofs (they are protected animals in Nepal). Next we went back to Patan to finish our shopping. There was a store where everything was hand-crafted in Nepal, including handmade paper.

I checked my baggage clear through to Chicago O'Hara airport and hoped I would see it again. As we were flying, we could see the mountains by moonlight. From Bangkok to Toyko, I received business class. But I couldn't see out the window. Most of the passengers looked like construction workers.

At Tokyo I said goodbye to Steve and Allison and spent about three hours at the airport. It was a beautiful day in Toyko and I enjoyed walking around. I had my last meal of the vacation in Japan. I still had my cough, but I could hope it would soon be over.

Over Alaska, I could see the mountain peaks through the clouds and then the clouds left and then I could see the snow-covered land. This was quite a bonus. When I landed in Chicago I was met by Lenora, Jacque, Jon and Adriene—and my luggage, much to my surprise.

I didn't climb the rest of the year, but did get to Devil's Lake with pictures of my trip. Looking back, we were lucky to have traveled so much in addition to our trek. I got to see and do much more than expected and I will never stop talking or thinking about my trip to Nepal.

TO BE CONTINUED

The next year, Lenora and I went to Turkey, so I didn't have a climbing trip. I was working long hours, even on Saturday.

In 2000, I went to Olive Ridge Campground in Colorado, by myself. When I got there, the ground was covered with snow, so I had to sleep in the back of the truck; however it did melt in a couple of days. My first hike was up to Chasm Lake. There was a lot of snow, but it was so hard I could walk on top of it. I wondered how many times I had gone up that trail in the years before. After spending about an hour, looking at the great East Face, I started back down. It took me almost as long to get down as it had to hike up, since I was so tired. Next day I went to Lumpy Ridge, with Jack Gorby and the rest of the climbers. We played this game, where you hop from one boulder to the next, without using your hands. The winner was the one that went the longest. I didn't win, but did pretty well.

Jack and the party were going to do a rock climb the next day, so I decided I would try to find the source of the Colorado River. After checking with the rangers, they could give me only a general direction where to start the walk. I drove over Trail Ridge Road and came to a spot they called Colorado River Trail Head. It is a well-marked paved trail since you go pass a ghost town called Lulu City, but since I was searching the source of the Colorado River, I bypassed it when I first saw it, and it was about twenty feet across. I crossed bridges back and forth, while it gets smaller and smaller. After about a four-hour hike, I came to a flat swamp area. There were many small streams and it was difficult to say which the main source was. This was truly a lifetime moment for me. To think, the mighty Colorado, the river that made the Grand Canyon, started amongst those tiny streams.

I took it easy on the way back down, going through forests of huge pine trees, with lots of Columbine and Indian Paint Brush. It may have been my imagination, but it seemed like things were different on this side of the divide. It seemed like the sun was brighter and the trees taller. I got back in time to eat supper with the rest of the climbers. The next day, I went to climb a named mountain so I could claim I had climbed mountains in seven different decades by the time I was seventy-two years old. I chose Hallets, since it was easy and almost 13,000 feet high. This is the one I had carried Jacque up to the top when she was three-years-old. I met Roger Weigon, again after nearly forty years, on the way up and we had a nice visit. After several rest stops, I was on top by noon. It was a clear day, so I could see for miles. Longs Peak looked entirely different from this angle. After about an hour, I began my descent. There were many people going up to Flattop, so the trail was crowded. It was hard to imagine, that this was the mountain we had climbed in a blizzard three years before. The next morning, all the climbers had a farewell breakfast at the Hummingbird Café at Allenspark.

Because I was still working on Saturdays, I didn't get to Devil's Lake that summer. But in 2001, our family (including Steve, Allison, Jacque and her husband, Matt, and grandchildren), camped at Coulter Bay in the Tetons. Jacque and her two-month old son, Caleb, slept in the van.

Lenora and I hiked around Two Ocean Lake (when they named this, they thought it was on the Divide where the water would go into the Pacific and Atlantic, but this didn't turn out to be true). On the way back, we saw a grizzly bear fishing off in the distance. Back at Coulter, the rangers stopped us at the entrance, and told us since we had left a cooler out in the open on a picnic table, we would be fined $100. It was a bitter pill, but they do that to keep the bears from roaming through the campground.

Steve and I wanted to climb a mountain while we were there, so we decided on Symmetry Spire. We could climb it in one day and wouldn't need a rope. We drove down to Jenny Lake, took the boat across to the start of the trail. After what seemed like countless rest stops, we finally made it to the top. I had been here several times, but I still got that great feeling of exhilaration when we were on top. This feeling I would describe as relief, fulfillment, and extreme happiness.

The way down was a disaster, since my right ankle turned to rubber and I was soon walking on the side of my foot. People were passing us right and left, probably wondering what was the matter. I finally found a walking stick, and we did get to the boat dock. The last boat left at six, so we were nervous that we wouldn't get there in time, but we did.

Lenora and I started home the next day, driving the truck loaded with all the camping gear, and stopped by Estes Park, and then took Route 36 home.

I went to Devil's Lake several times that fall. On the last rainy outing of the year, I had a group of first-timers underneath my dinning fly, trying to stay dry. Dave Ireland had invited the group and decided when the weather cleared; we would take the ten-mile hike to Parfeys Glen. On the way over, I noticed I had trouble going uphill. Parfeys Glen is a big canyon they have built wooden walks back into the cliffs. When you get to the end there is a large pool of water with a beautiful waterfall. The area took a lot of damage in the year of 2008, when a flood washed out the area and all the walkways. On the way back, I got farther and farther behind, but finally made it to camp.

When we got back home, I told my Doctor about it when I had my yearly physical. He had me take a stress test and found a blockage in my heart. I went to Saint John's Hospital in Springfield and they did a triple by-pass without having to stop my heart, and there was no damage. I always told Dave Ireland that the hike was what saved me from having a heart attack. After a short recovery period, I began therapy in at the Decatur Memorial Rehab Center in Sullivan. I trained very hard, so I was able to go back to Olive Ridge, with Jack Gorby's group in June of 2002. They were surprised to hear of my operation, but it is common now days and people get back to normal fairly quick.

Two years before, I had tried to get to Sand Beach Lake with snow-shoes, but finally had to turn around. This year there was no snow, so I was able to get to the Lake. I also climbed Estes Cone and Twin Sisters again. It felt good to get back to climbing. Jack Gorby was writing a book about the Stettners, and asked for my input. Lenora and I went up to a dinner meeting in Chicago, where he reviewed his book and I was mentioned several times.

At this dinner meeting, Amy Edwards came up and said, after that hike to Parfeys Glen, she and Dave Ireland became good friends and he taught her how to climb. The next year, every time they came to Devil's Lake, they would stop by my camp site, sometimes even for breakfast. I had retired by now so I would get to Devil's Lake four or five times a year. But soon after I learned that Dave had fallen to his death in the Bugaboos in Canada. He had dropped his camera and was attempting to rappel down to the camera, when he slipped. This was a great personal loss to me. I felt a special bond to him since we had been on the Parfeys Glen hike together that saved my life. I can only imagine how Amy and his parents felt, since they thought he was going on a fishing trip and then he died. When I climbed, I always knew there was a risk, but was willing to take it. I don't think I ever considered my family. In his honor, I built a bench for the Devil's Lake campfire, and many carved their initials in it.

As I write this and relive my climbing life, I have lived a miracle in timing. I was young in an era when climbing mountains was fairly new. I was able to climb with Europeans who had climbed the best. I had known the giants such as Paul and Joe Stettner, Hans Gmonser, Olle Swartling, George Porkney, Jim Toler. And I was blessed with friends that shared this interest such as Felix Hagerman, Peter Van Hook, my brother Gordon and many others. We formed a lasting bond all of us. During those years, it was possible to have first ascents on many mountains.

As I have grown older, my children have carried on the fascination of the mountains and the outdoor experiences. And this too added so much to a wonderful life. I couldn't have planned it and yet it all unfolded in a much better way than I could have ever imagined. I am reminded of that scene in the movie, *Pride of the Yankees*, when Gary Cooper says, "On this day, I consider myself the luckiest man on earth."

ABOUT THE AUTHOR

Rod Harris was born in the flatlands of Illinois. In 1948, at the tender age of twenty, he discovered the mountains and never stopped rediscovering them. He has climbed with the Chicago Mountaineering Club, seen death and danger, enjoyed Teton Tea Parties, camp life and the exhilaration of reaching summits in Colorado, Wyoming, Canada, Japan and Austria. At the age of seventy, Mr. Harris trekked to Everest. At eighty-one, he still enjoys the cliffs of the Wisconsin Dells and Devil's Lake with his children and grandchildren.